Understanding the Development of Small Business Policy

```
T0331442
```

It is not widely understood that the importance of small businesses only became apparent with the publication of David Birch's book *The Job Generation Process* in 1979. Over the past four decades, governments across the globe have struggled to design, implement and evaluate policies that benefit the development of small firms. Deciding whether macro or micro policies are more appropriate for a given context has usually created an initial challenge for policy-makers. However, a cause for even greater dispute has been determining and agreeing what might be the preferred outcomes of such policies (e.g. more firms, better performing firms, fewer firm failures, job creation, greater productivity, higher levels of innovation, inclusivity of disadvantaged groups). Furthermore, evaluating the impact of specific policies presents a wide range of difficulties since it is impossible to isolate a simple cause-and-effect relationship between policy and its stated goal. This book explores the development of small business policy in five countries across five continents and seeks to develop a deeper understanding regarding how small business policy has evolved in these countries and what we might learn from their experiences.

This book was originally published as a special issue of *Small Enterprise Research*.

Thomas M. Cooney is Professor of Entrepreneurship at the Dublin Institute of Technology, UK. He is also Policy Advisor to governments, the European Commission and international organisations, and has a strong publication record in the fields of entrepreneurship and small business. He is a director of several enterprises and works with commercial and not-for-profit organisations.

Understanding the Development of Small Business Policy

Edited by
Thomas M. Cooney

Routledge
Taylor & Francis Group

LONDON AND NEW YORK

First published 2019
by Routledge
2 Park Square, Milton Park, Abingdon, Oxon, OX14 4RN, UK

and by Routledge
52 Vanderbilt Avenue, New York, NY 10017

First issued in paperback 2020

Routledge is an imprint of the Taylor & Francis Group, an informa business

British Library Cataloguing-in-Publication Data
A catalogue record for this book is available from the British Library

ISBN 13: 978-0-367-58703-1 (pbk)
ISBN 13: 978-1-138-49687-3 (hbk)

Typeset in Minion Pro
by codeMantra

Publisher's Note
The publisher accepts responsibility for any inconsistencies that may have arisen during the conversion of this book from journal articles to book chapters, namely the possible inclusion of journal terminology.

Disclaimer
Every effort has been made to contact copyright holders for their permission to reprint material in this book. The publishers would be grateful to hear from any copyright holder who is not here acknowledged and will undertake to rectify any errors or omissions in future editions of this book.

Contents

Citation Information

The chapters in this book were originally published in the journal *Small Enterprise Research*. When citing this material, please use the original page numbering for each article, as follows:

Chapter 1
Entrepreneurship policy: issues and challenges
David Smallbone
Small Enterprise Research, volume 23, issue 3 (December 2016) pp. 201–218

Chapter 2
The evolution of public policy affecting small business in the United States since Birch
William J. Dennis Jr.
Small Enterprise Research, volume 23, issue 3 (December 2016) pp. 219–238

Chapter 3
The evolution of small business policy in Australia and New Zealand
Tim Mazzarol and Delwyn Clark
Small Enterprise Research, volume 23, issue 3 (December 2016) pp. 239–261

Chapter 4
Small and medium-sized enterprises policy in Korea from the 1960s to the 2000s and beyond
Chang-Yong Sung, Ki-Chan Kim and Sungyong In
Small Enterprise Research, volume 23, issue 3 (December 2016) pp. 262–275

Chapter 5
The financing of new firms: what governments need to know
David Storey and Julian Frankish
Small Enterprise Research, volume 23, issue 3 (December 2016) pp. 276–292

Chapter 6
Government agencies should be exemplars of business behaviour
Mark Allsop and Mark Brennan
Small Enterprise Research, volume 23, issue 3 (December 2016) pp. 293–301

Chapter 7

Colombia small- and medium-sized enterprise's 70 years of progress: what's next?
Rodrigo Otoniel Varela Villegas
Small Enterprise Research, volume 23, issue 3 (December 2016) pp. 302–315

Chapter 8

Does 'entrepreneurship' exist?
Simon Bridge
Small Enterprise Research, volume 24, issue 2 (August 2017) pp. 206–213

For any permission-related enquiries please visit:
http://www.tandfonline.com/page/help/permissions

Notes on Contributors

Mark Allsop is a Partner with Deloitte Private, based in Melbourne, Australia, where he leads the Commercial Advisory practice. He has over 20 years' experience as a management consultant and provides a broad range of support services to both private and public clients.

Mark Brennan was the inaugural national Small Business Commissioner, appointed by the Australian government. He advised the government on issues that impacted small businesses in Australia.

Simon Bridge is Professor in the Business School at the University of Ulster, Coleraine, UK. He has been involved in formulating, delivering and/or assessing enterprise policy for nearly 30 years, most recently as an enterprise and economic development consultant and before that as the enterprise director of a small business agency.

Delwyn Clark is Professor of Strategic Management at the University of Waikato, Hamilton, New Zealand. Her current research includes theoretical and applied projects on strategy models, entrepreneurial and innovation processes, business models and small- and medium-sized enterprise (SME) policies.

Thomas M. Cooney is Professor of Entrepreneurship at the Dublin Institute of Technology, UK. He is also Policy Advisor to governments, the European Commission and international organisations and has a strong publication record in the fields of entrepreneurship and small business. He is a director of several enterprises and works with commercial and not-for-profit organisations.

William J. Dennis Jr. is an independent researcher based in the USA. He was previously Senior Research Fellow at the National Federation of Independent Businesses Research Foundation.

Julian Frankish is affiliated with Barclays Bank. His chapter was written in a personal capacity.

Sungyong In is Managing Member of Ichthus International Law, based in Washington, DC, USA. He is a registered patent attorney in the firm's Intellectual Property group. He has extensive experience in telecommunications, software, semiconductor and electrical technologies.

Ki-Chan Kim is Professor of Business Administration and Dean of the Graduate School of Business at The Catholic University of Korea, Seoul, South Korea.

Tim Mazzarol is Professor in the Business School at The University of Western Australia, Perth, Australia. He has been actively engaged in consulting with a wide range of organisations from fast-growing small firms to large corporations and government agencies. Tim has undertaken over 200 projects in the areas of market research and economic or community studies for government and industry clients.

David Smallbone is Professor of Small Business and Entrepreneurship at Kingston University, UK. He has been involved in research relating to SMEs and entrepreneurship since the late 1980s, and one of his main research interests is entrepreneurship in transition economies. He is the editor of *Entrepreneurship, innovation and regional development* (2016, with Markku Virtanen and Arnis Sauka).

David Storey is Professor of Enterprise at the University of Sussex, Brighton, UK. He is the author of *Small Business and Entrepreneurship* (2010, with Francis J. Greene). His research is interested in all aspects of new and small firms, including finance, public policy, growth and entry and exit.

Chang-Yong Sung is based at the Seoul School of Integrated Science and Technologies, South Korea.

Rodrigo Otoniel Varela Villegas is based in the Centro de Desarrollo del Espiritu Empresarial at the Universidad Icesi, Cali, Colombia.

Introduction

Thomas M. Cooney

It is not widely understood that the importance of small businesses only became apparent with the publication of David Birch's book *The Job Generation Process* in 1979. This book highlighted that small businesses were the net creators of more jobs than large firms, and ever since governments across the globe have been struggling to design, implement and evaluate policies that benefit the development of small firms. Deciding whether macro or micro policies are more appropriate for a given context has usually created a significant challenge for policy-makers, but a cause of even greater dispute has been determining and agreeing what might be the preferred outcomes of such policies (e.g. more firms, better performing firms, fewer firm failures, job creation, greater productivity, higher levels of innovation, inclusivity of disadvantaged groups). Furthermore, evaluating the impact of specific policies presents a wide range of difficulties since it is practically impossible to isolate a simple cause-and-effect relationship between policy and its stated goal. This book explores the development of small business policy in countries with very different contexts and across five continents, plus it seeks to develop a deeper understanding regarding how small business policy has evolved in these countries and what one might learn from their experiences.

It has been highlighted that the Industrial Revolution changed many industries from craft production to mass production (Bridge and O'Neill, 2013). This change in manufacturing processes instituted a trend whereby government policy focused deeply on a small number of large manufacturing firms who were perceived to be the primary drivers of economic growth and would produce a 'trickle-down' effect. This concept of industrial policy was supported by the advent of 'scientific management' and the growth of Fordism (named after Henry Ford) which advocated the assembly line technique of mass production, supported by centralised administration. Within this economic perspective, the roles of small firms and new firms were largely overlooked. Stevenson (2008) suggested it was only after World War II that Small and Medium-sized Enterprise (SME) policies started to emerge because countries were seeking to stimulate national economies (e.g. Small Business Act, 1953, USA). Stevenson also propounded that the support measures introduced in the 1950s were primarily focused on access to finance but that in the 1960s the policies broadened to include competition law and antitrust policies with the ambition of bringing greater equity to the economic conditions influencing both large and small firms. The 1970s saw the focus change to developing SME management skills, and governments were now beginning to consider small firms as a different type of entity to large firms (e.g. Bolton White Paper, 1971, UK).

The debate regarding the value of small firms to the economy was fundamentally ignited by the publication of Birch's (1979) research on job creation in America between 1969 and 1976 which offered evidence that 66% of all jobs generated during the research period were created not by large organisations but by small businesses. The study has been widely criticised for its methodology, with Bannock (1981) remarking that the small firms in the study were defined to include subsidiaries and branches of larger enterprises, while Cordtz (1994) observed that if a firm employing, for example, 510 workers should make redundant 25 of them, then that firm became a small firm that had created 485 jobs. Work by Teitz et al. (1981) and Armington and Odle (1982) in the United States, and Storey and Johnson (1987) in Britain, argued that the figures presented by Birch were significantly overestimated. The notion of small firms being scaled-down versions of large firms was also challenged, an idea which Storey et al. (1987) viewed as being wholly inaccurate since several important distinctions exist, including the fact that there was much greater variability in the rate of growth and profitability amongst small firms. Kirchhoff and Greene (1995) observed that much of the disputation regarding small firms and employment generation had not been concerned with their level of positive impact, but instead the disagreement was engaged in methodologies. Additionally, while there was data in abundance to provide evidence of the ability of small firms to generate employment, the attention this topic received in the 1980s blinded many writers and researchers to several other issues. These issues included the continued impact of large firms on economic growth and the appropriateness of small firms as a panacea to unemployment. However, with the spotlight heavily concentrated on small firms, questions arose regarding how more ventures could be engendered and what type of people created them.

A 1995 Small Business Administration (SBA) report stated that approximately 53.7% of all payroll employment in the United States was in firms with fewer than 500 employees and that the greatest gains were in growing industries, with the highest percentage of employment in small firms. The report also noted the restructuring of American industry, with sectors traditionally dominated by large firms losing their overall employment share, while sectors that historically were the territory of small firms were now expanding. Other observations of the report included that small firms produced more than twice as many innovations per employee as large firms and that the continued strong stock market of the time had provided a stimulus to the initial public offering and venture capital markets for small dynamic firms. In the UK, Curran's (1996) examination of the revival of the small-scale enterprise suggested six factors that he believed had generated a perception of greater importance in small firms; primary among these was a rise in unemployment, an increase in outsourcing and the vertical disintegration of large enterprises. In Europe, the importance of small firms was also being noted in the 1990s. According to a European Observatory for SMEs Report (1995), the Europe-16 countries of 1990 (EU-12 and EFTA-4) had 16.4 million enterprises. Of these 93% employed less than 10 people and 6% employed between 10 and 99 people. Total employment in non-primary private sector enterprise was over 100 million, with micro-enterprises (<10 employees) holding 31% and small enterprises (10–99 employees) accounting for 25% of firms. The European Commission (1994) stated that in the European Union, firms employing less than 100 people constituted 99.4% of the total number of enterprises in the Member States. They also had the largest proportion of employees at 54.7% but a lower share of turnover at 47.1%. Figures such as these ensured that the enhancement and promotion of small firms was a priority throughout many of the economic policy decisions emanating from the European Commission and the Member States of the European Union.

Primarily because of the work of Birch (1979) and his assertions regarding the net job creation ability of small firms, the central focus of the economic impact of this sector became employment. Birley (1986) detected that new firms played a considerable role in creating employment, while Kirchhoff and Phillips (1988) determined that increases in small firm formation rates had a significant effect on net job creation. In Canada, Wannell (1992) also found that small firms were taking a bigger share of the employment market. In the UK similar findings were encountered as Doyle and Gallagher (1988) carried out an extension of the Gallagher and Stewart (1984) research and concluded that there was a consistent pattern in which small firms were net generators of jobs and large firms were net losers. However, they also discovered that while new firms and expansions of small firms were creating the jobs, a tendency existed to cease expanding employment once they had reached 20 employees. This is markedly different to the United States where the willingness to expand was diluted having reached 100 employees. The proliferation of studies on the ability of small firms to create employment encouraged a more blinkered vision of their overall contribution to the economy. Several researchers questioned the opinion that 'small is beautiful' and confronted what they viewed as extravagant claims about economic growth being fuelled by an increase in the number of small firms. Cordtz (1994) argued that firm size is not a useful predictor of employment gains or growth and that the underlying belief in small firms was being eroded by government small business schemes that had a mixed record. Cordtz additionally propounded that the jobs generated by small firms are not to the benefit of the worker, since they receive lower wages, poorer benefits and reduced job security.

Although the extent of the growth might be argued, the significance of small firms to a nation's economy had gained established recognition. And while the figures might be disputed, and each percentage point queried and re-evaluated, the central thrust of reports on both sides of the Atlantic Ocean remained the same – the small firm sector was an important constituent to engendering employment in any country. A Global Entrepreneurship Monitor Report (1999) found a strong positive correlation between high entrepreneurial activity (i.e. firm start-ups) and a country's economic well-being, particularly in terms of economic growth and job creation. Writers such as Brady and Voss (1995) praised the performance of small businesses in employment growth and in levels of innovation, success which they attributed to the heavy emphasis by SMEs on growth, their ability to respond quickly to change, their resilience and flexibility and their concentration on customer service. A common theme, therefore, throughout much of the commentary of the 1980s and 1990s was that small firms were potentially the primary solution to the question of job creation.

In more recent years, the emphasis on jobs has diminished somewhat as policy-makers now appreciate that small businesses also offer high levels of innovation and multiple other benefits to the economy. However, this has complicated policy-making even further as stakeholders are now asking if new policies should be seeking to achieve more firms, better firms, fewer firm failures, more jobs, less unemployment, higher productivity or help in overcoming disadvantage for targeted groups. Once the goal of a policy has been determined, the next question that needs to be addressed is whether that goal can best be achieved by macro or micro policies. An Organisation for Economic Co-operation and Development/ Eurostat framework for entrepreneurship indicators by Ahmad and Hoffmann (2008) suggested that the determinants of any policy should include the following categories: regulatory framework, market conditions, access to finance, research and development technology, entrepreneurial capabilities and culture. However, selecting from the menu of options under each category is challenging as each offer advantages and disadvantages, plus a host of unknown variables. The framework also suggested that the targeted entrepreneurial performance should be measured either by figures relating to firms, employment or wealth, while the impact should be measured by figures relating to job creation, economic growth, poverty reduction and the formalisation of the informal sector. With limited resources, a public that wants action but is unaccepting of failure, and a host of policy options that cannot be scientifically measured, it is little wonder that policy-makers are seeking evidence-based support to help them with their decision-making.

This book offers a deeper understanding of how small business policy has evolved in various countries on different continents. It provides insights for policy-makers and researchers regarding how small business policy is designed, implemented and evaluated, and suggests lessons from which relevant stakeholders can learn. The book opens by exploring the principal issues and challenges facing policy-makers, before then exploring the evolution of business policy in the United States, Australia, New Zealand and South Korea which assists the reader to appreciate how small business is influenced by different contexts (including culture). The book then takes one specific area (finance) and examines in a detailed fashion the impact of policy on this type of support. Next, two practitioners argue that government agencies should behave as exemplars for business behaviour, an ideal that raises many different issues. Then Colombia is used as a case study from which other countries can learn, before the book concludes with a provocative question: Does 'Entrepreneurship' Exist? The book is informative, enlightening and stimulating – enjoy!

References

Ahmad, N. and Hoffmann, A. (2008). *The OCED / Eurostat Framework for Entrepreneurship Indicators* – OECD Working Papers, OECD Publishing, Paris

Armington, C. and Odle, M. (1982). Small Business: How Many Jobs? – *Brookings Review*, Vol.1, pp 14–17

Bannock, G. (1981). *The Economics of Small Firms* – Basil Blackwell, Oxford

Birch, D.L. (1979). *The Job Generation Process* – Working Paper, MIT, Cambridge, MA

Birley, S. (1986). The Role of New Firms: Births, Deaths and Job Generation – *Strategic Management Journal*, Vol.7, pp 361–376

Brady, A. and Voss, B. (1995). Small is as Small Does – *Journal of Business Strategy*, Vol.16, No.2, pp 44–51

Bridge, S. and O'Neill, K. (2013). *Understanding Enterprise: Entrepreneurship and Small Business* – Palgrave Macmillan, Basingstoke

Cordtz, D. (1994). Small Is Beautiful – *Financial World*, Vol.163, No.9, pp50–55

Curran, J. (1996). The Role of The Small Firm in The U.K. Economy -*1st Midland Bank Small Business Lecture*, Kingston University, 6th June

Doyle, J. and Gallagher, C. (1988). Size-Distribution, Growth Potential and Job-Generation Contribution of U.K. Firms, 1982–84- *International Small Business Journal*, Vol.6, No.1, pp 31–55

European Commission (1994). *Panorama of E.U. Industry* – Office for Official Publications of the European Communities, Luxembourg

European Observatory for SMEs (1995) -*3rd Annual Report* – EIM Small Business, Netherlands

Gallagher, C.C. and Stewart, H. (1984). *Jobs and The Business Life Cycle in The U.K.* – Department of Industrial Management, University of Newcastle upon Tyne, Research Report No. 2, May (Revised 1985)

Global Entrepreneurship Monitor (1999). *Global Entrepreneurship Monitor Report* – Babson College, Wellesley, MA

Kirchhoff, B.A. and Greene, P.G. (1995). Response to Renewed Attacks on the Small Business Job Creation Hypothesis – *Frontiers of Entrepreneurship Research* (Editors: W.D. Bygrave, B.J. Bird, S. Birley, N.C. Churchill, M. Hay, R.H. Keeley and W.E. Wetzel), Babson College, Wellesley, MA, pp 1–15

Kirchhoff, B.A. and Phillips, B.D. (1988). The Effect of Firm Formation and Growth on Job Creation in the United States – *Journal of Business Venturing*, Vol.3, No.4, pp 261–272

Small Business Administration (1995). *The State of Small Business: A Report of the President 1994-* U.S. Government Printing Office, Washington, DC

Stevenson, L. (2008). Fostering Entrepreneurship – *35th International Small Business Congress*, Belfast November 2008

Storey, D.J. and Johnson, S. (1987). *Job Creation and Labour Market Change* – Mac Millan, London

Storey, D.J.; Keasey, K.; Watson, R. and Wynarczyk (1987). *The Performance of Small Firms: Profits, Jobs, And Failures* – Routledge, London

Storey, D.J. (1998). *Six Steps to Heaven: Evaluating the Impact of Public Policies to Support Small Businesses in Developed Economies* – Working Paper No. 59, Centre for Small and Medium-Sized Enterprises, Warwick University Business School

Teitz, M.B.; Glasmeir, A. and Svensson, D. (1981). *Small Business and Employment Growth in California* – Berkeley Institute of Urban and Regional Development, University of California, Working Paper No. 348

Wannell, T. (1992). *Firm Size and Employment: Recent Canadian Trends* – from: The Worklife Report, Vol.8, No.5, p 11.

Entrepreneurship policy: issues and challenges

David Smallbone

ABSTRACT

This article explores some current issues concerning entrepreneurship policy. It begins by examining the case for and against entrepreneurship policy followed by an analysis of the following issues: (1) the importance of context, which refers to the circumstances in which the policy was introduced and possibly maintained or modified; (2) the need for both researchers and practitioners to pay more explicit attention to the policy process which includes policy formulation, implementation, monitoring and evaluation; (3) the call for evidence-based policy in which it is suggested that what constitutes evidence is not always agreed between researchers, practitioners and policy-makers; (4) the need for a strengthened commitment to policy evaluation and (5) public procurement as an under-utilized type of policy intervention, yet one which is potentially very powerful.

Introduction

Since entrepreneurship has increasingly become a global phenomenon, so governments across the globe have paid increasing attention to it, or at least have claimed to have done so. Within this context, it seems appropriate to reflect upon some of the key issues raised by what is increasingly becoming a high-profile policy target. Whilst entrepreneurship results from the creativity, drive and skills of individuals, the actions of government and its policies are a key influence on the external environment in which entrepreneurship takes place (in some cases constraining it, in others facilitating it).

In initiating a discussion relating to entrepreneurship policy and some of the issues that need to be addressed if it is to be effective and appropriate in the future, the first task is to define what is meant by the term entrepreneurship policy. However, as in many other cases concerning entrepreneurship, there is not complete agreement between academics on this issue. On the one hand, researchers such as Lundstrom and Stevenson (2006) offer a relatively narrow definition which focuses on those policies specifically targeted at influencing entrepreneurship development. In this case, the question of what constitutes entrepreneurship policy is answered through a list of the types of policy interventions that are likely to promote and support it which include:

- The promotion of an entrepreneurship culture and more favourable attitudes towards entrepreneurship

- The integration of entrepreneurship education in schools and at all levels of post-secondary education
- A reduction in the barriers to entry, combined with pro-active measures to make it easier for enterprises to enter the market
- The provision of seed finance to facilitate business creation and subsequent development
- The various types of start-up business support including mentoring programmes, business incubators, designed essentially to increase the number of new businesses and nurture their early development
- Tailored effects to increase the participation in business ownership of under-represented groups, such as ethnic minorities, women and young people

In combination, such measures may be taken as an attempt to promote, encourage and support the development of entrepreneurship through various measures which are designed to improve the environment in which entrepreneurship can flourish.

In contrast, a more broadly based view of entrepreneurship policy is concerned with the effects of government policies and actions on the development of entrepreneurship, regardless of whether these are specifically aimed at entrepreneurs or not. Such an approach is best described as focusing on the government policies and actions that impact on the development of entrepreneurship, rather than focusing on policy measures that are specifically targeted at it. The point which needs to be stressed here is that whilst a narrowly defined entrepreneurship policy is only ever likely to affect a small minority of entrepreneurs and their businesses, there are a variety of types of policies and actions that government may engage in which affect most businesses. In practice a combination of these two interpretations of entrepreneurship policy may be required, with the Lundstrom and Stevenson (2006) emphasis being particularly appropriate in regions and countries where the level of entrepreneurship is at a low level. However, this does not negate the importance of active monitoring and review of the wider policy set as this needs to be done regardless of the current level of business start-up or business ownership. This broadly based view is represented by the work of Smallbone and Welter (2001).

Of course, there are good reasons why one would expect some variation between regions and countries in the types and strengths of policy intervention used, on the basis that the level of entrepreneurship itself can vary considerably between regions and between countries. Indeed, the attitude and stance of the population towards entrepreneurs also varies considerably at a regional and national level. Within this context, one would expect that where the level of entrepreneurship is low, more attention needs to be paid to the types of measures that are designed to promote it. In the so-called broad view of entrepreneurship policy, the central proposition is that the development of entrepreneurship is heavily influenced by the role that government plays in the macro-economic environment in which business is conducted. Of course, this argument applies rather more in mature market economies than it does in developing, or emerging, market economies, but nevertheless, government policies and actions impact on such indicators as exchange rates and interest rates which can have major impacts on the environment in which business is conducted.

A second element in the so-called broad view of entrepreneurship policy is identifying where government legislation and regulations impact on businesses, which is often argued to have a differential impact on businesses of different sizes (Kitching, 2006; van Stel, Storey, & Thurik, 2007). This is essentially a proportionality effect, with the impact on smaller businesses being stronger than in the case of larger enterprises where there may be an increasing managerial division of labour. This includes specialists taking care of some areas (such as health and safety), which in a firm of less than 20 employees will typically be one of the many responsibilities of the business owner. The argument here is not that government is 'out to get' the entrepreneur but generally the impact of its interventions include effects that were not intended.

The next influence is through the business tax regime, particularly in the case of economies that are at a lower level of development. For example, if one takes the case of the new member states of the European Union, these are countries which have operated under central planning in the past. In these countries, the employer's responsibility for social security payments in the early years of transformation was penal. The main problem was social security payments which during the Soviet period were the responsibility of state-owned enterprises. This meant that when the Soviet Union collapsed, many people were left without social security for a period. From a policy perspective, the problem was that there was no accumulated fund that could be used to kick-start the process of establishing a more centralized social security system and therefore the fund had to be built up from current income. The result was that it was almost impossible for small businesses to operate totally within the law and be profitable at that time. Consequently, many small businesses were forced into the informal sector for at least part of their activities.

The level of taxation was one problem for new member states of the European Union, but another was the frequent changes in tax regimes and taxation systems. In many respects, this was understandable given that these countries were finding their way in a market-oriented system, in which the role of government had fundamentally changed. But, from a business perspective, the rapid change in the tax regime and the expectations of the taxation authorities meant that many businesses found it necessary to employ accountants or taxation specialists to be compliant with these very frequent changes. The cost of supporting such staff was unnecessary in the minds of most small business owners; it was also a non-productive activity as far as they were concerned.

In making a distinction between so-called narrow and broadly based definitions of entrepreneurship policy, it would be wrong to give the impression that these are really alternatives. In practice, the emphasis made in the broad definition on monitoring all government policies and actions from an entrepreneurship point of view is essential whether or not the measures targeted at entrepreneurship are prioritized or not. In practice this is likely to be related to current levels of entrepreneurship and whether or not it is necessary to seek to kick-start a process of entrepreneurship development or lend support to a process that has started. One further definitional issue should also be recognized, namely, the distinction between entrepreneurship policy and SME policy. Although, in many cases, authors use these descriptors as alternative labels, in practice SME policy includes established businesses as well as new businesses whereas entrepreneurship policy emphasizes new business start-ups and entrepreneurial ventures within existing firms.

Following this introduction the case for and against entrepreneurship policy is briefly summarized. The rest of the paper is divided into five sections, followed by a conclusion.

The first section discusses the importance of context, which refers to the circumstances in which the policy was introduced and possibly maintained or modified. Context is a broadly based concept which includes social, economic, historical and particularly institutional environments. The second main theme is the need for both researchers and practitioners to pay more explicit attention to the policy process which includes policy formulation, implementation, monitoring and evaluation. The third theme is the often heard call for evidence-based policy in which it is suggested that what constitutes evidence is not always agreed between researchers, practitioners and policy-makers. The fourth theme refers to the need for a strengthened commitment to policy evaluation and the final key theme refers to public procurement which it is argued is an under-utilized type of policy intervention yet one which is potentially very powerful.

The case for entrepreneurship policy

In most cases, public policy aimed at promoting entrepreneurship is based on the premise that if entrepreneurs are to fulfil their longer-term contribution to society and economy, they may need some help particularly at start-up. This includes addressing some of the market failures they experience with respect to key resources such as finance, business information, advice and consultancy and premises.

The economic rationale for public policy intervention to support entrepreneurship development is captured in Figure 1. An enterprising SME sector means having SMEs that are growth-oriented and can impact on productivity, which is one of the key elements affecting competitiveness. As the diagram shows, SME growth can impact on GDP in three main ways: (1) through competition with other enterprises, (2) through innovation and (3) through what economists call productive churn which is the relationship between the productivity of businesses leaving the market in comparison with the productivity of new entrants. If the productivity of new firms entering the market is higher than those leaving, then there is a net gain in terms of the level of productivity in the economy overall. An additional argument in favour of entrepreneurship policy is to enable the potential contribution of entrepreneurship to social inclusion to be achieved.

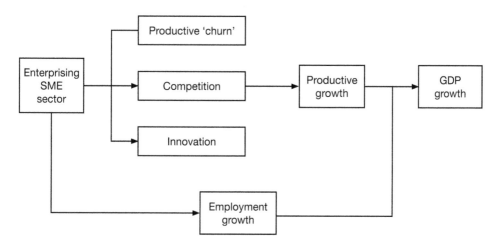

Figure 1. Entrepreneurship and economic development.

This is somewhat problematic as much of the evidence base to support the proposition that entrepreneurship reduces social inclusion is not robust.

One of the underlying themes that run through the paper is the need to recognize the context in which entrepreneurship policy is developed and introduced. This applies in the case for entrepreneurship policy insofar as this is affected by current levels of business start-up and business growth. It can also be used as part of the argument against maintaining or increasing entrepreneurship policy. This is an argument developed by Bennett (2008) who suggested that in the UK (for example), most of the market failures that have been used as a justification for policy intervention in the past, have now either been rectified or are close to being rectified, and consequently, it is no longer appropriate to have a comprehensive programme of support for entrepreneurs.

The case against entrepreneurship policy

The ineffectiveness of much of entrepreneurship policy is one of the main reasons why it has come under increasing criticism. Clearly the effectiveness of policy in achieving its objectives can be determined by the implementation mechanisms that are used because, no matter how well designed a policy is, if the agents responsible for delivering it do not have the confidence and penetration of the target group, it is unlikely that the policy will be effective. Moreover, policy implementation can become unnecessarily complex, thereby contributing to confusion in the minds of the target group, particularly in terms of the number of sources of help and advice that are available. If a lack of clarity exists in terms of which agencies are responsible for what (and when), then the target group will lack confidence in the providers of the support and the policy is unlikely to be effective.

The low level of awareness of public policy measures appears to be a universal phenomenon. Even in countries such as the UK, where the infrastructure for the implementation of public policy with regard to entrepreneurship is reasonably well developed, there are target groups that are difficult to reach by mainstream support agencies. In this regard, there are different models of policy delivery. One is where government organizations are responsible for delivering the support themselves. An alternative model is where the delivery is contracted out to other organizations, which has both advantages and disadvantages. It is usually a method for reducing costs, particularly overhead costs. The contracting-out model can be effective if the agencies that are delivering the contract have strong roots with the target group they are aiming to serve. Examples include different types of ethnic minority groups, where a specialist agency in ethnic minority enterprise is likely to have more penetration of that sector than mainstream agencies.

The evidence available to help assess the effectiveness of public policy is quite limited, even in the UK where some form of entrepreneurship policy has been in existence for many years. An analysis of the period 1999–2009 showed little evidence that entrepreneurship policy has resulted in either an increase in business start-ups or an increase in growth amongst existing firms (Bennett, 2008). This lack of evidence has contributed to an emerging view of the ineffectiveness of entrepreneurship policy mainly, perhaps, because of the ineffectiveness of its implementation. The reasons why implementation often falls short, or is less effective than it should be, includes situations where policy is formed without consideration of implementation issues. Another reason is that there is insufficient consultation with the target group about the methods of implementation. Additionally, frequently there are insufficiently clear policy goals and a lack of skill on the part of those responsible for the policy implementation to be successful.

Critics typically attribute the lack of effectiveness of entrepreneurship policy to the way it is implemented. At the same time, Shane (2009) has suggested a more fundamental explanation for its lack of effectiveness, namely that it represents bad policy. Storey (2000) had made a similar point, suggesting that entrepreneurship policies that are currently pursued often lack clear objectives. But recent analysis suggests that bad policy results from the way that it is formulated (Dennis, 2011). So, it is fair to say that, hitherto the policy formulation stage of the policy process has not attracted a lot of attention from entrepreneurship and small business researchers. This is an area where one must be critical.

In the private sector, the starting point for the development of a new product or service would include some market research. This might include focus groups where those most affected by the new product would have an opportunity to express their view. In contrast, throughout the world it is extremely rare for policy-makers to formally engage with the stakeholders (i.e. small business owners) about policy design and policy delivery. This is one area where there is a need for improvement if the effectiveness of public entrepreneurship policy is to be increased. There is something to be learned from the Chinese in this regard, where a degree of policy experimentation is employed. This may involve testing a policy approach in some cities before the policy is rolled out across the country. Arshed, Carter, and Mason (2014) argued that a key factor explaining the ineffectiveness of entrepreneurship policy is how it is formulated. The process of policy formulation is seldom visible to those outside government departments and has been largely ignored by previous research. Within this context, their research showed that in interviews with senior policy-makers, the policy-makers showed an awareness of how the formulation process should work ideally, whilst recognizing that the reality is somewhat different. Therefore, Arshed et al.'s research opens up new challenges for future research as more evidence is needed to better understand the processes involved in entrepreneurship policy formulation (e.g. who the key actors are and what is the role of ministers and senior civil servants is in this process?).

The question of policy effectiveness also needs to be considered in relation to the cost involved. There is a need for more research because there have been few attempts to fully assess the costs of entrepreneurship policy to the tax payer. The UK government attempted to do it and in Europe a research project known an Institute of Innovation and Entrepreneurship has also sought to do this. However, cost benefit analyses of this sort are difficult because of the need to measure benefits and costs that are hidden. Nevertheless, the results of a UK government investigation by the Department of Trade & Industry in 2003 were staggering. Aggregate expenditure on entrepreneurship policy was estimated to be between £8 and £10 billion at a time when expenditure on police services and on the universities, was slightly lower at around £7 billion in each case. Moreover, the expenditure involved came from a wide range of government departments, not simply the department that was mainly responsible for enterprise policy. Unlike other major spending areas, such as the police and universities, expenditure on entrepreneurship policy was not the responsibility of a single ministry or department making it more difficult to control. The key spending department was the Treasury, where spending on entrepreneurship policy, particularly through tax relief was valued at £2.6 billion in 2002, increasing to £3.6 billion in 2006. The results were surprising; firstly, because of the sums involved, which can be explained by the fact that much of it was in the form of tax relief from other forms of subsidy; and secondly, because the organization mainly responsible for delivering small business policy at the time, namely the Small Business Service, only accounted for approximately 2.5–3% of total expenditure. So, when the ineffectiveness of the policy field is combined with its large cost, this helps to explain why in recent times there has been a growing number of questions asked about the true value of this policy area.

Key issues for entrepreneurship policy

Policy issue no. 1: increasing attention should be paid to the context for entrepreneurship policy

One of the emerging themes in the literature on entrepreneurship in recent times has been a call for a more explicit emphasis on context which, in the case of some theoretical approaches, has been rather neglected hitherto. Context refers to the historical, social, economic and institutional environment and their interrelationship into a complex and unique whole (Welter, 2011). However, just as context is important for the study of entrepreneurship, it is also important for a study of entrepreneurship policy.

Since the needs, strengths, weaknesses, threats and opportunities facing countries, regions and localities vary, so the context in which entrepreneurship may be a potentially positive influence on the development of these areas also varies. More specifically, the context for entrepreneurship policy includes the current level of entrepreneurship and the trends within it. This is likely to impact on the needs of the region, locality or country with regard to attempts to stimulate more entrepreneurial activity. It is also influenced by the characteristics of these areas which may have an impact on how easy or difficult it is for entrepreneurship to take on this role. All these features are important if the polices that are developed and prioritized are to make an effective contribution to economic development within the areas of which they are a part.

In addition, a consideration of context is vital where policy transfer is considered a part of an approach to economic development policy. The potentially controversial nature of this exercise is reflected in the substantial literature that has been devoted to it. Issues that arise include what exactly should be transferred? Is it the concept and/or the method of implementation? Or is it the whole package? The latter approach is unlikely to be effective unless the institutional framework in the recipient region or country is compatible with that in the source area. This applies, not just to the formal institutional frame but also the informal one, in the sense of how these institutions behave.

Within this context, and not surprisingly perhaps, attempts to transfer policy from Europe to China have proven to be particularly difficult (Atherton & Smallbone, 2013). This is not altogether surprising in view of the substantial differences between the cultures in terms of their institutional frames. Once small business ownership was made legal in China and, having established a network of loan guarantee institutions across the length and breadth of the country, the Chinese government decided to turn its attention to business development services (BDS). This is partly because entrepreneurs often need help in writing business plans to support their funding applications.

The development of BDS was considered complementary to the financial interventions and the Chinese government turned to those parts of the world where the provision of business advice and consulting for small businesses was well established. This included some technical assistance projects, including one that focused on designing a strategy for the provision of SME support in China. The consultancy team working on this project included the author of this paper, whose responsibility was to design a BDS model that could be adapted for cities at different levels of development (Smallbone, Xiao, & Xu, 2008). To undertake this task, surveys were conducted with providers of business development services and with businesses that were potential users of BDS. These surveys were designed and implemented in co-operation with local officials in each city to demonstrate an evidence-based approach to policy formulation. Some people have argued that China does not need to follow the business support systems that are typically found in mature market economies, such as the UK, the USA and Germany. This is partly because China has developed informal support systems which are close to the entrepreneur, both in physical distance and in the way in which the relationship is perceived by business owners.

Some authors have argued against encouraging China to develop the kind of formal business support services network that has been attempted in many European countries either in the form of Chambers of Commerce or public and semi-public sector agencies, such as Business Link in the UK. However, whilst such methods may have served Chinese businesses well in the past, there is a question whether these informal institutions are suf- ficient to meet the needs of an emerging private sector in the future. It is the view of the Chinese government that they are not. Continuing reliance on the informal systems of the past is unlikely to provide enough access to the business services that they need to help them to upgrade their management practices and widen their resource base. This particu- larly applies in the case of small enterprises. A subsidized consulting scheme was devised for the Chinese economy and it was targeted at small businesses which had not previously used external consultants, whether for the development of strategy or more operational matters. The idea is that if the public sector subsidizes the first round of consultancy use, and if the consultants delivering the advice and support are vetted and accredited, then there should be double benefit. On the one hand, the market for consulting by small businesses is widened and on the other, there is an increase in the number of con- sultants who have experience of working with small businesses.

Clearly therefore, the percentage of the total consultancy costs that are subsidized is central to the question of the extent to which the measure incentivizes business owners to make use of consultants. This is how such schemes operate in Western countries where this type of measure has proven to be quite successful. However, in China, the financial support from central government for a policy such as this is only forthcoming when there are some results. In other words, the financial support is retrospective. Clearly this represents a very different philosophy and is problematic in the case of sub- sidized consultancy because, in the Chinese model, potential participating businesses do not know what the level of subsidy will be when they are expected to commit to the pro- gramme. This uncertainty makes it difficult to recruit small businesses for the programme.

A further example of the difference between the Chinese and Western contexts is with respect to the encouragement of growth in small businesses. In Western countries, the prin- ciple is the one applied above, namely, to identify businesses that are trying to grow and to offer financial assistance to help them to deal with some of the issues and constraints that they face to help them achieve the growth they seek. By contrast, in China, the financial support appears to take the form of a prize that is given to businesses that achieve growth, once growth has been achieved. From a Western perspective, there appears to be little additionality in this model but, instead, a substantial portion of deadweight. Critics may suggest that these differences should have been identified by the consultants from the outset. This may be the case, but on the other hand, there were other quite significant differences which were identified and addressed. The lack of strong centrally organized consultant accreditation system is one example. One might expect the local officials to have pointed out these issues but they did not. More generally one might suggest that transferring policies between contexts with such a wide, cultural and institutional divide will inevitably throw up problems. Clearly, the difference in the nature and behaviour of institutions is at the heart of this.

Another situation where context is important refers to the neighbours of the European Union, such as those who aspire to become members of the European Union (Xheneti & Kitching, 2011). The contextual issue in this case refers to the lack of responsiveness of those responsible for transferring policy to local conditions, the lack of appreciation of the need to identify the strengths and the weaknesses, not just in the economy and the business community, but amongst practitioners and those in government responsible for developing policy. Without this, it is unlikely that the policies that emerge will be well tuned to the needs of the economy.

Policy issue no. 2: greater recognition should be given by researchers and practitioners to the importance of the policy process

The study of public policy typically disaggregates the policy process into a number of components. Figure 2 from Young and Quinn (2002) represents a conceptual model of the policy cycle. The diagram demonstrates that research has the potential to influence the process at any stage, although the nature of the research required may vary. Sutcliffe and Court (2005) summarized the main stages as: (1) agenda setting, which refers to

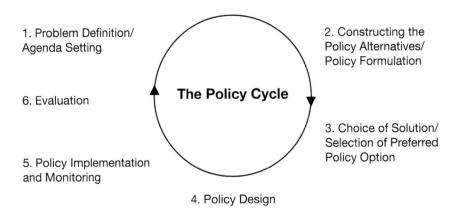

Figure 2. The policy cycle.
Source: Young and Quinn (2002).

the awareness of and priority given to a particular issue; (2) policy formulation, which refers to the ways, options and strategies are constructed; (3) policy implementation, which refers to the forms and nature of policy administration and the activities associated with it and (4) monitoring and evaluation of policy.

Breaking down the policy process into different stages enables a more analytical approach to be used with regard to the effectiveness of policy, the evidence requirements and policy at different stages, the influence of implementation on the effectiveness of policy, and, as Arshed et al. (2014) emphasized, it also draws attention to the process of policy formulation. Clearly entrepreneurship policy has increasingly been criticized for its lack of effectiveness and there are different views regarding the reasons for such outcomes. Arshed et al. (2014) and others have emphasized the way in which policy is formulated, although this specific stage is seldom visible to those outside of government departments and has largely been ignored by previous research. Arshed et al.'s groundbreaking work was based on a period of internship in the Ministry responsible for SME and entrepreneurship policy development. Her interviews with policy-makers indicated that, whilst they are aware of how the formulation process should work ideally, they recognize that reality was rather different. The period of participant observation led Arshed to the conclusion that the policy process was distinguished by a lack of transparency and a lack of procedure. A key point in Arshed's analysis is the role of what she describes as institutional entrepreneurs who are 'autonomous and reflective agents wreaking havoc on established orders as they create new social entities' (Aldrich, 2011, p. 1). Because entrepreneurship literature is predominantly focused on implementation and evaluation (Mole, 2002), the formulation stage has largely been ignored, which is where Arshed's study makes a significant contribution. What her internship enabled her to do was not simply to describe the so-called institutional entrepreneur, but to provide detailed descriptions of what they do. Arshed's work opens new challenges for future research which includes more evidence to better understand the processes involved and the role of key actors, particularly the role of ministers in relation to senior civil servants.

However, it is important to recognize that generalization from the study should be made with extreme caution because any policy needs to be considered in relation to the context in which it is formulated and developed. Arshed's investigation represents the situation at a specific point in time. Since then the individuals in government may have changed because of elections and some individuals may have just may been moved to different posts. It is the process that needs to be generalized rather than the detailed content. The other comment to note is that the study was limited to one stage of the overall policy process. One of the intentions is to develop future research and explore more fully other stages of the policy-making process (e.g. engaging with policy influencers or understanding better the implementation phase). Nevertheless, this research plugs a gap in the policy literature through paying attention to the formulation stage which previously had been relatively neglected.

Policy issue no. 3: more explicit attention should be paid to evidence-based policy

Using evidence to inform policy is not a new idea, although it has increased in emphasis in the UK over the last 15 years or so. The term came into greater prominence during the period of the Blair Administration and was intended to indicate the entry of a government with a modernizing mandate. Essentially evidence-based policy may be viewed as part of a rational and systematic approach to policy-making. It is based on the premise that policy decisions should be better informed by the evidence available rather than just informed opinion (see Figure 3). Although the concept grew in prominence within the UK, arguably its significance is particularly important in developing countries where it is typically less well established. It is suggested by some that better utilization of evidence in policy can help to reduce poverty and save lives (Sutcliffe & Court, 2005).

At the same time, the use of evidence-based policy does raise some issues. One is the nature of the evidence that should be used in the policy-making process where the literature tends to emphasize the breadth of evidence, combining robust academic research with evidence provided by stakeholder groups and others. The second issue is how evidence is incorporated into policy-making. Policy processes typically involve different stages from setting the policy agenda, to policy formulation and to policy implementation. It may be argued that evidence has the potential to influence the policy-making process at each stage, although the evidence used may be different at each of the policy stages, and thirdly, evidence is not the only factor which influences policy-making. Perhaps the most important point here is that, whilst academics may look for a more logical and rational process, the political pressure is typically to process information quickly, leading to a recognition that policy-making is neither objective nor neutral. It is a political process.

Sutcliffe and Court (2005) refer to a hierarchy of evidence which means that, although forms of evidence may share equal importance in theory, in practice they do not. Since not all forms of evidence share equal weighting, attempts have been made to identify the key characteristics of evidence that influence whether or not it is used (Shaxson, 2005). The first criteria are quality, accuracy and objectivity. There are issues related to the objectivity of the evidence and its sources. Clearly, any bias in the evidence base needs to be identified in order that it can be considered when interpreting the evidence for policy. The second criterion is credibility as Shaxson (2005) suggests that credible evidence relies on a strong and

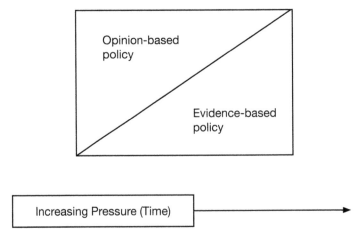

Figure 3. The dynamics of evidence-based policy.
Source: Adapted from Gray (1997).

clear line of argument, tried and tested analytic methods, and analytic rigour throughout the processes of data collection, analysis and on the conclusions. It is very difficult for policy-makers to check evidence so they tend to rely on the reputation of the sources of proxy. The third criterion is relevance. The key issue here is that evidence is timely, topical and has policy implications. Lastly, practicalities, which relate to the extent to which the evidence is accessible to policy-makers and in what form they can access the findings as well as the evidence base.

Figure 4 provides a generic description of the flow of evidence in the policy process. Despite its simplistic nature it offers a number of important insights. Firstly, it provides a similar distinction between agenda setting, formulation and monitoring and the different evidence collection processes needed. Secondly, it raises a distinction between evidence needs for pressing policy decisions and those for longer-term strategic policy objectives.

In Table 1 as Sutcliffe and Court (2005) demonstrate, the nature of the evidence required varies at different stages of the policy process. They make the point that experience with evidence-based policy in mature market economies cannot be simply transposed into developing countries, which typically have a diverse set of economic, social, economic and political environments, or whose capacity is more limited and whose resources are scarcer. Therefore, evidence-based policy approaches will need to be adapted if they are to be effectively used in tackling each of the above in turn and beginning with different types of evidence. It may be argued that what counts as evidence varies as much from the researchers' work in practice to the end use of the evidence.

One of the reasons why it may be argued that evidence-based policy matters, particularly in the field of international development, is because these are fields where the decision-maker has largely been flying blind as robust evidence is simply not available.

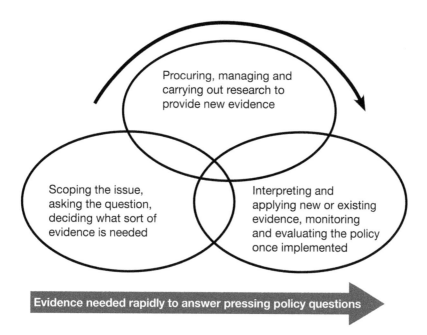

Figure 4. The flow of evidence in the policy process.
Source: Shaxson (2005, p. 104).

Table 1. Components of the policy process and different evidence issues.

Stage of the policy process	Description	Different evidence issues
Agenda setting	Awareness and priority given to an issue	Evidence of new problems or the magnitude of a problem so that relevant policy actors are aware that the problem is important. A key factor is the credibility of evidence but also the way evidence is communicated.
Formulation	There are two key stages to the policy formulation process: determining the policy options and then selecting the preferred option (see Young & Quinn, 2002, pp. 13–14)	For both stages, policy-makers should ideally ensure that their understanding of the specific situation and the different options is as comprehensive as possible. This includes the instrumental links between an activity and an outcome as well as the expected cost and impact of an intervention. The quantity and credibility of the evidence is important.
Implementation	Actual practical activities	Here the focus is on operational evidence to improve the effectiveness of initiatives. This can include analytical work as well as systematic learning around technical skills, expert knowledge and practical experience. Pilot projects are often important. The key is that the evidence is practically relevant.
Evaluation	Monitoring and assessing the process and impact or an intervention	The first goal is to develop monitoring mechanisms. A comprehensive evaluation procedure is essential in determining the effectiveness of the implemented policy and in providing the basis for future decision-making.

Source: Adapted from Pollard and Court (2005).

The argument may be applied in the case of entrepreneurship and its contribution to social inclusion. It may also be applied to research on clustering. In both these cases it can be argued that policy has run ahead of the evidence base. Clearly academics have a potential role in relation to public policy to contribute evidence to support or question important policy areas. This certainly applies in the case of entrepreneurship and it also applies in the case of international development.

In the UK, the Regulatory Policy Committee represents an attempt to implement evidence-based policy more systematically than previously. This Committee provides government with external independent scrutiny of evidence supporting changes in law that affect businesses amongst others. The Committee is sponsored by the Department for Business Innovation and Skills and comprises eight independent experts drawn from a variety of backgrounds. The Committee was established in 2009 and represents the first body in the UK established to provide independent scrutiny of proposed regulatory measures put forward by government. The Committee assesses the quality of evidence and analysis supporting regulatory change and its potential impact on businesses. They check the estimated costs or savings to businesses as the result of regulatory reform that is put forward by central government departments. They check that government departments explain new regulation including comparison with other possible alternatives namely, voluntary codes of practice.

When new regulations are required, the Committee then checks that government is minimizing the effect of any negative impact on small businesses amongst others. The approach involves providing opinions on the impact, assessments submitted by the government department responsible. The underlying rationale for this policy initiative is to seek to ensure that policy and decisions are made based on accurate evidence, and the

Committee provides advice on the quality of the available evidence. Issues of evidence-based policy have been dealt with essentially as a technical problem. However, policy-making is very much a political process and as Figure 5 suggests, many factors compete with the evidence base to take centre stage in policy formulation. Indeed, it should be noted that some writers think it is a mistake to utilize a evidence-based policy approach as this tends to result in the policy process being seen as being primarily focused on technical issues, a highly political dimension to it at as well.

Policy issue no. 4: a strengthened commitment should be made to policy evaluation

Another issue requiring more attention in the future is policy evaluation, particularly the evaluation of policy impacts. Although the UK is often seen as a leader in policy evaluation with the ROAMEF reference (rationale, objectives, appraisal, monitoring, evaluation, methodology) as a blueprint, in practice it would seem that the limited resources made available to gather evidence as part of policy evaluation means that the systematic implementation of policy evaluation is less than ideal. In practice the emphasis tends to be on low-level monitoring (counting numbers in other words) of businesses supported and those growing, but without a more rigorous evaluation of policy impact. As far as the actual process of policy evaluation itself is concerned, it may be criticized as being too narrowly based on quantitative approaches when the addition of a qualitative dimension could help to give more insight into how and why a policy can be made more effective.

Policy evaluation studies have been identified as one of the most rapidly developing areas of entrepreneurship policy-related research (Gilbert, Audretsch, & McDougall, 2004). One of the challenges facing policy evaluators is the diversity of policies that are designed to encourage and support entrepreneurship. These include some that apply to

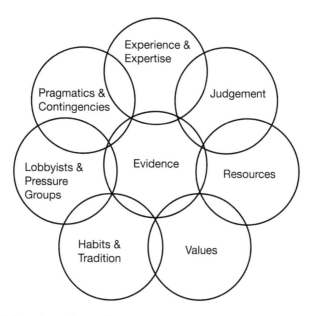

Figure 5. Factors influencing policy-making in government.
Source: Davies (2004).

all types of enterprise, but also others that are focused on specific types of enterprise, such as firms of explicit size, sector or growth potential. This diversity also applies to various types of assistance which, in some cases, can be very light (such as requests for information) and, in other cases, more intensive (such as one or more advisory sessions). One of the problems with the former is that often entrepreneurs find it impossible to recall an event that may not have been sufficiently important to them to retain in their memory.

One of the most significant contributions to the field of the policy evaluation studies is the work of Storey (2000, 2002) whose so-called 'Six Steps to Heaven' has been used to describe and assess the approaches used to undertake monitoring and evaluation of policy. His 'Six Steps to Heaven' start with simple monitoring and end with highly sophisticated evaluation methods. One of the problems with these evaluation studies is the difficulty of finding appropriate data on which to base the evaluation. Whilst government departments may announce their intention to build evaluation into policy design, this is rarely translated on the ground to delivery organizations collecting the kind of information that the policy evaluators require. However, some of these studies can be criticized because the data are used as a basis for what are often sophisticated econometric methods although the data are not always fit for purpose. Storey's Six Steps are summarized as follows. Step 1 is the take up of schemes. Step 2 looks at recipient's opinions about schemes. Step 3 involves recipient's views of the difference made by the assistance they have received. Collectively the first three steps Storey describes as monitoring. Step 4 involves a comparison of the performance of assisted recipients with typical firms. Step 5 involves comparison with matched firms and Step 6, which is the most sophisticated, considers selection bias. Steps 4–6 Storey describes as evaluation because all of them attempt to determine the economic impact of the policy initiatives.

Policy issue no. 5: greater attention should be paid to the use of public procurement as a policy tool

Procurement refers to the acquisition of goods, services or works from an external source. It is found in both public and private sectors and, in the latter case, corporations are involved. These processes are intended to promote fair and open competition, whilst minimizing exposure to risk. In the UK, the most commonly used definition of procurement by UK government departments are taken from the Gershon (2004) review of procurement in central government in 1999. Gershon (2004) stated that procurement refers to the entire process of acquisition from third parties (including the logistical aspects) and that it covers goods, services and construction projects. The procurement process can involve several stages. For example, it may include a bidding process known as tendering, as the organization requiring a product or service may set a threshold above which the contract must go out to competitive tendering. The latter is a noteworthy feature relevant to public sector procurement. Such an invitation to tender will contain a statement of what is required by the purchaser. Within the European Union there are strict rules on public procurement which have been set and which public bodies must follow. Ultimately procurement, whether by public sector organizations or corporations, represents a significant market opportunity for SMEs. Therefore, whether there is a level playing field (or not) with regard to access is an important issue. The EU threshold above which all public contracts are subject to EU rules is important because, for micro-enterprises and for those enterprises that are owned by members of minority groups, it is likely that contracts below this threshold will be more relevant to them. Although procurement contracts represent a market opportunity for SMEs, the problem is that for the smallest businesses there are typically deficiencies in the market for procurement contracts that operates to their disadvantage.

One reason why public procurement warrants attention is its sheer scale. This is easy to understand when one considers the fact that public procurement is undertaken by central government departments and ministries, regional authorities, local government, public sector hospitals, schools and so on. Gordon Brown, as former prime minister of the UK, once remarked that if a government could increase the procurement contracts going to small and medium-sized businesses by 1%, everything else that is done for small firms would look insignificant. It has been argued previously that the greatest potential for developing public procurement as a public policy tool lies at the local government level because of the responsibilities that local authorities have for their constituents. But what type of measures are needed if public procurement is to be more accessible by small and medium enterprises is answered in the way that contracts are packaged and specified. An organization's strategy for making a procurement process more open should be based on the following elements:

- Reaching potential suppliers through publicizing its procurement requirements using a combination of the internet, advertising in conventional media and 'meet the buyer' events
- Packaging contracts in ways that encourage potential suppliers to bid (this will involve training its own staff to modify their approach)
- Enabling suppliers to bid by helping them to meet the eligibility criteria

As well as opening-up public procurement to SMEs, in general there have also been attempts to use public procurement as a policy tool with regard to the minority and more disadvantaged groups. Such initiatives are known as supplier diversity programmes and typically involve three main elements: (1) organizations that are interested in diversifying their supply base; (2) businesses from minority groups that are interested in increasing their capacity to win public sector contracts and (3) a business support agency to assist in building the capacity of the purchasing organizations as well as the potential suppliers and organizing 'meet the buyer' events. This is an area that is well worth developing further. Moreover, there is enough good practice around to inform such a programme.

Conclusions

It must be stressed that this paper represents work in progress, particularly the part that is concerned with future policy issues and policy priorities. As it stands, the selection of priorities and challenges is rather idiosyncratic, with some major themes left untouched with targeting is a good example. A key underlying theme in the paper relates to whether entrepreneurship policy is necessary and, if so, what form it should take and how it should be delivered. The conclusion at this stage of the research is that entrepreneurship policy is not essential to the needs of the economy and of society. However, neither is it a red herring. Context is the key. Many factors influence the role and importance of entrepreneurship policy and specifically the level of development and the current level of entrepreneurship development.

One of the factors influencing one's answer to this question is 'What is understood by entrepreneurship policy?' In the case of countries where the level of entrepreneurship development is medium-to-high in international terms, one might suggest that the type of entrepreneurship policies described by Lundstrom and Stevenson (2006) no longer look necessary. However, at the same time, it is necessary for government to monitor its own legislation and actions if entrepreneurship is not to be constrained by a regulatory regime that requires a significant effort on the part of businesses to understand and adapt to. So, in other words, one cap does not fit all and differences in context between countries and, in some cases between regions, is essential to understanding the role and importance of entrepreneurship policy. The growth of interest in the policy process reported above should be built upon and become a focus for entrepreneurship policy-related research in a way that it has not done so in the past. It has been argued previously that one of the positive influences of EU membership on entrepreneurship policy in the New Member States was the need to recognize and adhere to the EU's agenda as policy-makers in New Member States were forced to review their policy processes and practices. A precise example would be to link explicit strategy with an action plan and, most importantly, with a budget. This has helped to address what previously had been a significant problem in these countries, namely a so-called implementation gap.

In addition, research on the policy process could provide a focus for other aspects of what is suggested in this paper; for a stronger commitment to evidence-based policy, for example. One of the issues that some people who read this paper will be thinking is, where does this leave academic researchers interested in public policy, and what are the implications for the nature and extent of their contribution? Another underlying theme emerging from the review concerns the limited use by entrepreneurship policy researchers of developments in other policy areas. This is a mistake because, in some cases, issues or topics are coming onto the agenda for entrepreneurship policy have been analysed and discussed by colleagues in other policy areas in the past. This is exactly what happened in the case of a study of mainstreaming undertaken by Blackburn and Smallbone (2008). This study was concerned with the circumstances in which a group of policy measures that had been developed and implemented in the case of a targeted initiative (often an EU funded initiative) analysing to what extent could such measures be mainstreamed (in the sense of being rolled-out across the country) and what conditions were necessary to influence their effectiveness? Research for this study showed that, 10 years previously, very similar questions would have been asked in relation to social policy and health policy. Whilst the context may be different, clearly there are potential dangers in following this kind of line too narrowly. Nevertheless, in reviewing some of the factors influencing whether or not mainstreaming is appropriate, remarkably similar discussions and applications were found in the health and social policy area. In this regard, this is an area which needs to be given more attention in the future as another policy transfer field, whilst paying attention to differences in context.

References

Aldrich, H. E. (2011). Heroes, villains and fools: Institutional entrepreneurship, not institutional entrepreneurs. *Entrepreneurship Research Journal, 1*(2), 1–6.

Arshed, N., Carter, S., & Mason, C. (2014). The ineffectiveness of entrepreneurship policy: Is policy formulation to blame? *Small Business Economics, 43*, 639–659.

Atherton, A., & Smallbone, D. (2013). Promoting private sector development in China – The challenge of building institutional capacity at the local level. *Environment and Planning C: Government and Policy, 31*(1), 5–23.

Bennett, R. (2008). SME policy support in Britain since the 1990s: What have we learnt? *Environment and Planning C: Government and Policy, 26*(2), 375–397.

Blackburn, R., & Smallbone, D. (2008). Researching small firms and entrepreneurship in the UK: Developments and distinctiveness. *Entrepreneurship Theory and Practice, 32*, 267–288.

Davies, P. (2004). *Is evidence-based government possible?* Jerry Lecture presented at the 4th Annual Campbell Collaboration Colloquium, Washington, DC.

Dennis, W. J., Jr. (2011). Entrepreneurship, small business and policy levers. *Journal of Small Business Management, 49*(1), 92–106.

Gershon, P. (2004). *Releasing resources for the front line: Independent review of public sector efficiency*. Norwich: HMSO.

Gilbert, B., Audretsch, D. B., & McDougall, P. P. (2004). The emergence of entrepreneurship policy. *Small Business Economics, 22*(3–4), 313–323.

Gray, J. A. M. (1997). *Evidence-based healthcare: How to make health policy and management decisions*. New York, NY: Churchill Livingstone.

Kitching, J. (2006). A burden on business? Reviewing the evidence base on regulation and small-business performance. *Environment and Planning C: Government and Policy, 24*(6), 799–814.

Lundstrom, A., & Stevenson, L. A. (2006). *Entrepreneurship policy: Theory and practice*. New York: Kluwer Academic.

Mole, K. (2002). Business advisers' impact on SMEs: An agency theory approach. *International Small Business Journal, 20*(2), 139–162.

Pollard, A., & Court, J. (2005). *How civil society organisations use evidence to influence policy processes: A literature review* (ODI Working Paper 249). London: ODI.

Shane, S. (2009). Why encouraging more people to become entrepreneurs is bad public policy. *Small Business Economics, 33*(2), 141–149.

Shaxson, L. (2005). Is your evidence robust enough? Questions for policy makers and practitioners. *Evidence and Policy: A Journal of Research, Debate and Practice, 1*(1), 101–112.

Smallbone, D., & Welter, F. (2001). The role of government in SME development in transition countries. *International Small Business Journal, 19*(4), 63–77.

Smallbone, D., Xiao, J., & Xu, L. (2008). Developing the small business market for business development services in Chengdu: Policy issues and priorities. *Journal of Small Business and Enterprise Development, 15*(4), 656–674.

van Stel, A., Storey, D. J., & Thurik, A. (2007). The effect of business regulations on nascent and young business entrepreneurship. *Small Business Economics, 28*(2), 171–186.

Storey, D. J. (2000). Six Steps to Heaven: Evaluating the impact of public policies to support small businesses in developed economies. In L. Sexton & H. Landstrom (Eds.), *The Blackwell handbook of entrepreneurship* (pp. 176–194). Oxford: Blackwell.

Storey, D. J. (2002). Methods of evaluating the impact of public policies to support small businesses: The Six Steps to Heaven. *International Journal of Entrepreneurship Education, 1*(2), 181–202.

Sutcliffe, S., & Court, J. (2005). *Evidence based policy making: What is it? How does it work? What relevance for developing countries?* Overseas Development Institute.

Welter, F. (2011). Contextualising entrepreneurship: Conceptual challenges and the way forward. *Entrepreneurship Theory and Practice, 35*(1), 165–184.

Xheneti, M., & Kitching, J. (2011). From discourse to implementation: Enterprise policy development in post-communist Albania. *Environment and Planning C: Government and Policy, 29*(6), 1018–1036.

Young, E., & Quinn, L. (2002). *Writing effective public policy papers: A guide to policy advisers in central and Eastern Europe*. Budapest: LGI.

The evolution of public policy affecting small business in the United States since Birch

William J. Dennis, Jr.

ABSTRACT
This paper assesses the evolution of public policy affecting small business in the United States both in terms of content and process since the 1979 publication of David Birch's *Job generation process*. It focuses on four major trends – a change in the prevailing policy agenda, the increasing use and importance of carve-outs, the failure to distinguish between small and entrepreneurial business for policy purposes, and the rise and subsequent ebb in small business's political influence. The paper concludes that the small-business agenda and policy affecting it will continue to evolve with a divide in the priorities among small business and technology-oriented business as one major political party will tend to champion the former and the other will tend to champion the latter.

A ripe atmosphere

The public policy impact of David Birch's work *Job generation process* is difficult to exaggerate and impossible to measure (Birch, 1979). Yet, Birch's work did not start the process that eventually led to a revised policy agenda and the political rise of small business. Both were already underway, making the *Job generation process* a catalyst/accelerator rather than an author, speeding, intensifying, and focusing subsequent developments in policy affecting small business instead of creating them.

By the late 1970s, an entrepreneurial "something" was in the air. The exponential growth of listings under the headings "small business" and "entrepreneurship" in the Reader's Guide signaled the public's rising curiosity in the phenomenon (Dennis, 1993). Simultaneously, student interest budded as entrepreneurship (and small-business management) courses at colleges and universities grew from a trickle into a stream. Information technology was beginning to blossom and major industries, such as trucking, were deregulated, providing new opportunities for entrepreneurs. The *Economist*'s 1976 Christmas cover story, written by its deputy editor, Norman Macrea, was titled "The coming entrepreneurial revolution" (Macrea, 1976). Macrea's assessment seemed prescient, but was probably not. The coming entrepreneurial revolution was likely already upon us. Underscoring the point – the small-business job generation phenomenon that Birch documented drew its data from events prior to Macrea's article.

The policy/political arena also began sniffing that entrepreneurial "something". Both chambers of the U.S. Congress elevated modest subcommittees of their respective Banking Committees to full Small Business Committees in 1974 with legislative authority. An unobtrusive Office of Advocacy was administratively established within the U.S. Small Business Administration (SBA) for the purposes of promoting policy ideas that would advance small-business interests, an office that would become far more substantial when Congress legislated it in 1976. The first White House Conference on Small Business since the Roosevelt Administration was held four years later. The U.S. Regulatory Council (1981), an extension of the White House, identified 43 examples of carve-outs, that is, different rules for large and small businesses, existing in 1981. The nation's largest small-business organization, the National Federation of Independent Business (NFIB), began computerizing its 600,000 member membership list by industry, geography and issue opinion (J. Motley, personal communication, March 28, 2016), a move that would yield it enormous, if temporary, political advantages compared to other interests throughout the 1980s and into the 1990s. The Reagan Revolution with its emphasis on enterprise moved into the White House in early 1981, representing an attitude change that was years in the making.

When Birch (1979) published his findings, the policy atmosphere was ripe to embrace them, and it did. The setting was as if the *Job generation process* provided a reason to do what many already wanted to do. Small business could now be an economic centerpiece, and by extension a political centerpiece, not because it had always been the "little guy" and enormously popular with the public, in lore if not always in practice,[1] but because it created jobs. "Jobs" was the political elixir then and remains so today.

The following pages discuss the evolution of policy affecting small business in the United States from publication of the *Job generation process* to the present. It argues that its evolution appeared in four important ways – a change in the prevailing policy agenda; the expanding use of carve-outs to account for operational differences in large and small firms; the failure to distinguish small from entrepreneurial business as objects of policy; and, the rise and subsequent ebb in small business's ability to influence the content of policy affecting it. Brief examples illustrate basic points. Space limitations prevent discussion of either evolutionary trends or examples in detail, and require their confinement to the Federal government in a country where states and localities exert considerable influence over small-business affairs.

The agenda shift

Perhaps the most prominent and certainly the most important change in American small-business policy occurring since Birch is an agenda shift, that is, a basic change in the type and mix of policy issues recognized as small business relevant. Prior to 1980, small-business policy issues largely involved questions of support and shelter.[2] Policy equated to subsidy for one or more segments of the population; the corollary was protection from larger competitors. The creation of SBA, an off-spring of efforts to save small manufacturers from the post-World War II slowdown in demand for military hardware, is the prime example. Attitudes changed notably as the contents of Birch's research spread. Small business was no longer viewed as the helpless orphan, pummeled by a turbulent, unforgiving environment; rather, it was viewed as an economic contributor. Yes, small business still faced difficult competitive struggles. But, it now offered more than nostalgia; it offered something concrete and current; it offered jobs. The more closely policy-makers looked, the more they noticed small business offered other useful things as well, innovation being a prime example. Support and shelter questions quickly fell away to be overtaken by questions of more effective means to stimulate small-business contributions. Small-business owners eagerly told all willing to listen how to do that. In response, the policy emphasis transitioned from government supports and shelter to reduction in government impediments.

The small-business voice

The 1980 White House Conference on Small Business yielded a policy blueprint drafted by small-business owners themselves (White House Commission on Small Business, 1980). The delegates'[3] priority recommendations focused on impediments that crossed business-size and industry-sector boundaries. Recommendations and priorities from the 1986 and 1995 Conferences followed suit (White House Commission on Small Business, 1986, 1996). (No Conference has been held since.) Changed circumstances resulted in occasional different emphases, such as a swap-out between inflation and liability insurance issues between the 1980 and 1986 gatherings. Delegates focused on capital formation (particularly tax), regulatory reforms, employee-related issues, and broad economic concerns such as government spending and balanced budgets. Support and shelter issues did occasionally rise to the priority list. A prime example occurred in the 1986 Conference when the 13th recommendation (out of 60) called for retention of SBA as an independent entity. However, the sentiment appears a reaction to the Reagan Administration efforts to pare, if not eliminate, the agency. The vote likely expressed backing for a small-business voice within government, rather than support for the programs the agency administered.

The White House Conference assessments of small-business owners' views on policy issues was broadened and extended in a series of nine membership surveys conducted by the NFIB Research Foundation between 1982 and 2012 (Dennis, 2009a).[4] While this survey series focused on problems rather than solutions, as had the Conferences, it yielded outcomes paralleling Conference recommendations and priorities.

The series of NFIB surveys is not isolated. The National Small Business United, for example, a much smaller organization with a membership more favorable to support and shelter efforts (based on the issues its officers express interest in), found the same emphasis among its membership (National Small Business Association, 2014). In 2014, for example, 64% thought reducing and reforming taxes would help their businesses and a non-mutually exclusive 58% thought just getting government out of the way would be helpful as well. Fourteen percent cited more assistance programs as useful.

Small-business owner policy priorities have been clear for years and the policy/political community generally followed its lead. The obvious argument in support of the proposition is the outcome. The agenda could not have shifted without policy-makers buying-in. Example evidence for the agenda shift can be found in the hearing schedule of the U.S. House of Representatives' Small Business Committee. The Committee's legislative authority is restricted to SBA with its panoply of support and shelter programs. However, rules and custom allow the committee and its subcommittees to conduct investigative (fact-finding) hearings on small-business topics, including aspects of legislation under other committees' jurisdiction. The Small Business Committee and its subcommittees do so extensively, particularly when compared to hearings conducted on support and shelter activities (its official jurisdiction). That is not to imply committees of jurisdiction then ignore small business. To the contrary. In early 2009, for example, hearings on what would become the Affordable Care Act (Obamacare) were just beginning. As part of the kick-off process, the six-person panel testifying before the Ways and Means Committee[5] on employer-provided health insurance included two small-business witnesses, a human resources executive from IBM, an assistant to the President, the AFL–CIO, and two researchers from policy organizations (U.S. House of Representatives, Committee on Ways and Means, 2009).

The new policy agenda had several important consequences. It affected virtually every small business in the country rather than the relative handful affected by support and shelter programs. It challenged the interests of traditional political powerhouses, requiring small business to fight increasingly difficult policy battles and to become increasingly political. And, it contained an overarching ideological perspective – eliminate government impediments to success rather than provide subsidies to help create success – that was not welcome in all quarters, including among some small-business owners.

Issues that never appeared

Two issues areas that appeared ripe for small-business policy development in 1979 were competition (anti-trust) and finance. Both wilted. The cause of the former is more difficult to understand than the cause of the latter. The most visible competition legislation specifically designed to shelter small business from predatory competition was the Robinson–Patman Act of 1936, sometimes known as the "Magna Carta of Small Business".[6] A refugee of the Great Depression, the Act still enjoyed considerable support in the Congress and among segments of the small-business owner population into the late 1970s (Bauer & Kintner, 1986), prior to Birch's publication and concurrent with the initial phases of Wal-Mart's explosive growth. The era of massive retail chains and the destruction of small retail firms was well underway[7] and the competition issue appeared primed to move to the fore. It never did. John Satagaj, an influential and active participant in small policy matters for over 30 years, was just one knowledgeable observer surprised by the turn-of-events on competition questions. He noted with a sense of incredulity that the Small Business Legislative Council (SBLC) to which he was General Counsel had a strong anti-trust (competition) committee when he assumed his position in the mid-1980s, only to see the committee abandon by the early-mid-1990s (J. Satagaj, personal communication, March 19, 2016).[8]

The prevailing anti-trust policy in the United States protects competition, not competitors (Kolasky, 2004). Robinson–Patman is now typically viewed as sheltering incumbents rather than protecting consumers. The Federal Trade Commission's opposition, before the District of Columbia Taxicab Commission, to local cab company efforts to rein in entrepreneurial Uber underscores the point (Lerner, 2013).

Still, a significant percentage of small-business owners, somewhat less than one in 10, continue to consider "competition with big business" to be their single most important business problem (Dunkelberg & Wade, series). In industries such as retail, the proportion is even higher. Yet, that business problem did not translate into policy issues and viable solutions. The competition issue emerging from the White House Conference of 1980, in fact, was not predatory activity of chain stores, but the non-taxed "unfair" competition that government(s)' and non-profits' commercial activities posed (White House Commission on Small Business, 1980).

The reason for non-activity in this policy area is difficult to explain. Perhaps it is the joint interest of large firms and consumers conspiring to ensure the lowest possible selling price regardless of its implications for small business. Perhaps it is the ideological acceptance of economies-of-scale as legitimate and any malpractices it conceals to be coincidental. Perhaps the issue area is simply too complicated and the instances too isolated to matter. One observer simply attributed the de-emphasis on competition questions to changed conditions (Anglund, 2000). The socio-economic problems of job creation and innovation displaced the old competition problem. With the serious inflation of the 1970s and early 1980s putting a premium on depressing consumer price increases, and the simultaneous international competitiveness issues which accentuated a need for greater firm efficiency, the latter explanation proves as good as any.

Finance, principally debt finance, is the second policy area that never developed into a central small-business issue. Borrowing concerns did arise during recessions, the more serious the recession, the greater the concern. But, they typically evaporated once the following expansion set-in. Poverty groups raised micro-finance issues. Yet, they were modest and peripheral. Venture finance found its problems with regulatory agencies, such as the Securities and Exchange Commission. Sarbanes/Oxley of 2002, for example, designed to improve financial disclosure to protect investors from accounting fraud, created a massive accounting cost and paperwork burden for small publicly held firms and those wishing to become one (Carpenter & Rowe, 2005). Raising venture finance per se was never a serious problem; excess in late 1990s and early 2000s was.

Small-business finance in policy parlance typically means access to business loans. Two reasons explain why loans never developed into the policy issue that taxes, for example, did.[9] The first was deregulation of the financial services industry and the resulting satisfaction of most small-business loan demand, at least until recently. The Great Recession and the failure of small business lending to rebound as in past recessions may transform bank lending into an important small-business policy issue in the future, but that certainly does not characterize the prior 30 years (Mills & McCarthy, 2014). The second reason is the substantial population of small-business owners who do not want to borrow. That, too, reduces the number potentially wanting to make small-business lending an issue.

Deregulation of Depression-era banking restrictions in the 1980s and 1990s generally resulted in a more favorable borrowing climate as bank competition for small business's banking business progressively rose (Dennis, 2008). A series of surveys showed perceived competition for small business's banking business steadily climbing from 1980 through 2006. At the beginning of the period, for example, a net (greater competition minus less competition) 8% found more bank competition for their banking business compared to three years earlier. A quarter century later the figure stood at a net 33% (Dennis, 2008).[10] The result was that small business access to credit was extraordinary. The Federal Reserve reported that in the mid-2000s, 87% who applied for new credit obtained it (Board of Governors of the Federal Reserve System, 2007). Those figures were somewhat higher than the still very high percentage it reported five years earlier. Another nationally representative survey conducted among small employers in 2006 yielded similar numbers

(Scott & Dunkelberg, 2005). The discouraged borrower phenomenon was not addressed in these studies, but was not likely to have changed the results appreciably. The mid-2000s appears to be a high point. Figures following the Great Recession show about half now obtaining the loans requested (Dennis, 2012; Federal Reserve Banks of New York, Atlanta, Cleveland and Philadelphia, 2014). However, sources other than commercial banks have risen recently to augment finance availability.

The second reason that access to loans has not been an issue is that a significant number simply do not want loans, or want them infrequently. These owners may be credit averse or simply in a financial position where business loans are of no interest to them. If an owner does not want a loan, access is not a problem. The size of that group is elusive and likely varies over time. We do know that somewhat over 60% in the early 2000s had some type of business debt outstanding (Board of Governors of the Federal Reserve System, 2007); in 2005, 52% had not requested a loan in the prior three years; (Scott & Dunkelberg, 2005); and, immediately following the Great Recession, 43% had not wanted to borrow in the last year of which 7 percentage points classified themselves as discouraged borrowers (Dennis, 2012). Loan demand has subsequently returned to pre-Recession levels (Federal Reserve Banks of New York, Atlanta, Cleveland and Phila-delphia, 2014). Still, the number not in the market remains reasonably large, depressing lending as policy issue.

Institutionalizing carve-outs

Economic research dating at least to the mid-1980s establishes that regulatory compliance has a disproportionate impact on small business (Brock & Evans, 1985, 1986; Hopkins, 1995). Compliance therefore results in a competitive disadvantage for small firms. The reason for the disparity is that regulatory compliance demands both fixed and variable costs; spreading fixed costs over fewer units of output tilts the impact against small businesses. A little-noticed factor underlying the economic disparity is that government crafts administrative regulations to fit the most complex practices of the most complex organizations. That means many (most) small-business owners find rules do not fit their operations, are incomprehensible, or both. The alternative to tailoring rules for the most complex is for policy-makers to tailor them for fit the least complex. That approach leaves the most complex, usually large firms, to run amok. Neither approach therefore efficiently nor fairly reaches regulatory objectives.

These economic and political realities, coupled with Birch's findings and a competitive 1980 election, caused policy-makers to find a way around the disproportionate negative consequences of single rules. Their solution was carve-outs, an inelegant term describing a series of possible actions that makes rule compliance for small business easier than it otherwise would be. Carve-outs effectively make two sets of rules, one for small firms as defined by the carve-out and one for others. While neither an ideal solution for the dis-proportionate impact problem nor logically consistent with often strongly held views about equal protection of the laws, the principle seems to have been accepted – if for no other reason than it is the best in a series of poor alternatives.

The first major post-Birch manifestation of the principle was the Regulatory Flexibility Act of 1980.[11] It was hardly the first instance of a legislative carve-out. But, the Regulatory Flexibility Act was important because it institutionalized and legislatively legitimized the principle, though it would be inconsistently applied outside the legislation's parameters. The Regulatory Flexibility Act has evolved significantly since its passage. The evolution was principally stimulated by one legislative action, the Small Business Regulatory Enforcement and Fairness Act (SBREFA) of 1996, and one administrative action, Executive Order 13272 of 2002. The effect of both was to strengthen the ability of SBA's Office of Advocacy, the organization charged with enforcing the Act, to more effectively exert the powers granted it by giving the Office authority to take non-complying agencies to court, demanding agencies to internally establish procedures to implement the Act's requirements, and requiring the Office to create a formal training program to help those writing rules and making economic analyses to understand their responsibilities under the law. While small-business proponents still point to weaknesses, the Act has unquestionably evolved over the last 35 years into a more powerful and helpful body of law.

The most recent annual data show that the Office saved small entities (via the Act) an estimated $1.6 billion (Office of Advocacy, US Small Business Administration, 2016), a rather modest amount historically (Dennis, 2009b).[12] It even publically identified one scofflaw, the Fish and Wildlife Service at the Department of the Interior, a highly unusual public rebuke of a fellow agency. However, the original intent of the Act was not so much to directly make measurable regulatory savings or publicly shame recalcitrant agencies. Rather, it was to encourage agencies to write rules that consider small business from the outset, as the rules are being written without need for Office of Advocacy intervention (Dennis, 2009b). The Office's training function has therefore evolved into a major activity over the last decade, an activity which in retrospect should have begun immediately after the Act's passage. A change in mindset among regulation-writers (the ultimate goal) is difficult to measure, but Tom Sullivan, a former Chief Counsel for Advocacy, observed one critical, positive trend (T. Sullivan, personal communication, April 8, 2016). Meetings of the American Bar Association's Administrative Law section in the early 2000s had scant attendance when the session focused on regulatory flexibility, and participants regularly ridiculed the Act. Today, those meetings are packed with eager participants because, according to Sullivan, they see that regulatory flexibility results in better rule-making.

The Affordable Care Act of 2010

The carve-out principle appears most significantly directly in legislation. The small-business exemption to the mandatory health insurance provisions of the Patient Protection and Affordable Care Act of 2010, known as Obamacare, and the Section 179 expensing provisions of the Internal Revenue (IRS) Code illustrate the point well. Both are recent, have an enormous impact on small business, were rational political responses to conflicting policy demands,[13] and occurred after significant, and in the case of the latter, lengthy political debate. They are examined one at a time.

The primary concern of small-business owners during debate over Obamacare was the cost of health insurance, and by extension a potential requirement, typically called "the mandate", that all employers offer (and pay a large share of) health insurance to their employees. The cost issue was important to all businesses. The coverage issue mattered only to small-business owners as more than 95% of employers with 50 employees or more already offered insurance; fewer than half with less than 10 employees did (Kaiser Family Foundation & Health Research & Educational Trust, 2015). Small business opposed the mandate. It made two basic arguments to support the position. The first was that those businesses currently offering employee health insurance had the financial wherewithal to do so while those without the financial wherewithal were the ones not offering. A significant new burden would submerge the most marginal businesses along with their employees. The second argument and the one generally accepted by proponents as well as opponents of the proposed health care reform is that many smaller, small businesses would simply pass their mandated health insurance premiums back to employees in the form of lower pay and benefits (Emanuel & Fuchs, 2008; Summers, 1989). Since most not offering health insurance pay relatively low wages, the mandate would result in fewer jobs and/or stagnate or lower wages for the poorest paid employees. Because of such outcomes, policy-makers driving the proposal decided to exempt those employing fewer than 50 people, effectively carving-out from the employer-mandate provisions more than 95% of the employer population covered by the Patient Protection and Affordable Care Act of 2011 (Obamacare).

The foregoing example illustrates several points relative to the present discussion. First, the carve-out appeared in a significant piece of legislation, the most consequential of the Obama presidency and one of the most important in recent American history. The appearance of a singled-out small-business interest in the 1970s on such an important matter would have been highly unlikely. Second, small business created considerable political difficulties for proponents. If small-business job creation were threatened as small business argued, the proposal's job consequences could damage the economy, a prospect that threatened the proposal's legislative outlook (recall, this debate occurred in 2009 and 2010 when effects from the Great Recession were still omnipresent). The carve-out allowed proponents to tell constituents that small employers were not affected by the legislation. It proved an effective, if somewhat disingenuous, argument. Third, 50 employees is an arbitrary carve-out level as are all carve-out levels. But, it has virtues. Nearly all employers who employed more than 50 people already offered health insurance. The trade-off, then, was maximum employee health insurance coverage with minimum employer complaint.[14] Fifty employees as a limit was also simple, a nice round number, easy to understand and follow.[15]

Section 179 expensing

The second carve-out example involves tax, a policy area that probably has created more sustained interest among small-business owners than has health. Depreciation for tax purposes is more than an accounting exercise. It means real dollars for the businesses affected, both in terms of taxes paid and the accounting costs accompanying them. Expensing, an immediate deduction of qualified assets for income tax purposes, is effectively a form of accelerated depreciation. Its dual advantages for those who can use it are simplicity, including a considerable paperwork reduction, and a one year write-off of most newly purchased tangible business assets.

Section 179 expensing now allows business owners to expense up to $500,000 in qualified assets (virtually all tangible assets, except most new construction) purchased during a tax year. The tax benefit begins to phase out at $2 million and ends completely at

$2.5 million, thereby limiting its availability to smaller firms. Expensing was first introduced in 1958 at $2000 and largely forgotten until 1981 (U.S. Congress Joint Committee on Taxation, 2015). The Economic Recovery Tax Act of 1981 began a lengthy and tortuously winding path to expensing of most small-business capital investments. A major purpose of the 1981 Act was to accelerate business depreciation in order to enhance capital formation and investment. But it soon became evident that large and small businesses would effectively be treated very differently by the proposed new Accelerated Cost Recovery System (ACRS). Small businesses could not use the highly complex ACRS system as a practical matter. To compensate, Congress raised the expensing limit to $5000 with gradual increases to $10,000 scheduled over the next five years. For the following three and one-half decades, the size of the expensing limit periodically and significantly changed (up and down). While never lapsing, small-business owners often were not certain if Section 179 benefits would be available when they wanted to invest. Content unpredictability compounded transience. Asset coverage changed, though the range was generally expanded throughout. Thirty-four years after the small business expensing policy became part of the small-business agenda, it became a permanent portion the tax code, buried by friendly legislators as a small provision in the "must-pass" PATH Act of 2015. Expensing was challenged throughout the process on two fronts: the first was competition for available resources. The dollars available for tax cuts are limited with many powerful interests competing for them. Small business was just one of those interests, and it was often conflicted having other tax issues in which it was interested as well. The second challenge was economic efficiency. Section 179 expensing was justified in part as a stimulant to small-business investment. But did it really accomplish that objective? Considerable opinion was not so sure (Guenther, 2015).

The Section 179 carve-out contains similar and dissimilar characteristics compared to the Affordable Care Act. Both were part of significant political struggles involving the nation's most powerful interests, the former extending for a considerable period and the latter occurring more intensely and in a compacted time frame. Both came in high-profile issue areas. Both affected large numbers of small businesses, vastly more than any support program could. However, their triggering mechanisms differed notably. The carve-out for Section 179 expensing was defined by investment size rather than the more typical employment size as found in the Affordable Care Act. Policy-makers considered the amount of investment a more appropriate proxy for small business in this case than employment or some other measure. Simplicity for tax-payers and tax administrators was an obvious reason for its selection. However, the ratio of investment to employees differs enormously across industry resulting in notably different concepts of small business in the two examples. The lack of a small-business definition in the United States facilitates such differences (Dennis, 2015).

Small-business owners and entrepreneurs

Birch was clear that small business created a disproportionate share of the net new jobs in the United States over the period he examined (1969–1976). He was also clear that a disproportionate share of jobs small businesses created were produced by a modest subset of small businesses he called, gazelles (Birch, 1979, 1987). The public, including most policy-makers, quickly absorbed Birch's first message; it largely ignored the second. The result was that entrepreneurial business and small business were undifferentiated in most policy quarters well into the l990s and in a large number of them to the present. That made the policy agenda for small business and entrepreneurial business one and the same.

A related point of obfuscation also pervaded the policy community from the days following publication of the *Job generation process* to the present. Birch pointed out that gazelles, that is, entrepreneurial businesses, appeared in all industry sectors; they were not isolated in a few industries. Yet, even the cognoscenti usually failed to distinguish between entrepreneurial businesses and (high) technology businesses. High-tech businesses may or may not be entrepreneurial just as non-technology businesses may or may not be. Adding to the obfuscation is the place of business starts, particularly when they are the next pizza carry-out or lawn service provider. Are these new entries entrepreneurial endeavors, and if so, when do they cease being entrepreneurial? Recent research highlights the importance of new firms (vs. small firms) in the job generation process (Haltiwanger, Jarmin, & Miranda, 2010). This new information elevates the significance of starts in small-business-oriented policy, and raises concerns as their number is falling (Haltiwanger, Jarmin, & Miranda, 2012). Yet, it is not clear where new starts fit in policy development and what policy can do to stimulate their formation. Little policy addressed or addresses new formations, with the exception of the Enterprise Zone concept dating back to the early 1980s (Butler, 1981). Incubators, many of which now have a technology-orientation, also do. However, incubators involve relatively few starts compared to the population and tend to be state and local activities (beyond the scope of this paper), sometimes drawing on Federal funding for support.

None of the distinctions outlined above became policy significant after the *Job generation process*'s publication. Small business was the umbrella that essentially covered all. The Small Business Investment Company program (SBIC) operated by SBA did (and does) indirectly target its modest resources on entrepreneurial and technology-oriented firms (https://www.sba.gov/sbic, 2016).[16] The Small Business Innovation and Research (SBIR) program created in 1982 draws a specified minimum percentage from the large research budgets of 11 major government departments and agencies to develop commercially viable goods/services; the program's running mate, the smaller and newer Small Business Technology Transfer program is similar, but requires small-business collaboration with research institutions. Though SBIR remains highly popular, all mentioned in this paragraph are reminiscent of the support and shelter programs that have virtually disappeared from the small-business agenda.

A flurry of activity in technology policy over the last decade or so reversed the relative calm of the prior years. Much of that flurry focused on establishing or changing the rules of the game. The pace of technological change in areas from information to the biological sciences had simply outstripped government's capacity to deal with it. The changes obviously impacted small businesses, both as technology providers and as technology consumers. Issues in technology policy frequently politically pit industry against industry and/or technology against technology. Small and entrepreneurial businesses, in those instances, often line up with their large firm, industry counter-parts. A major exception is patent policy, an issue that had languished for more than half of a century. It tended to pit large against small. The America Invents Act (AIA) of 2011 was the first major change in American patent law since 1952. The greatest alteration it made was switching from the first-to-invent concept to the first-to-file, aligning the U.S. system more closely with the rest of the world (Mattappally, 2012). Small-business interests were not happy with the change and opposed the legislation, but lost to a seemingly simpler system favored by the multi-nationals. As a sop to small firms, two carve-outs dealing with a grace period for filing and filing fees became part of the law. While still too early to assess the veracity of small-business concerns, the Canadian experience with a similar transformation decades earlier is not encouraging (Lerner, Speen, & Leamon, 2015). Unfortunately, the AIA did not settle matters. Rather, it led to a host of new issues that are likely to stir the policy kettle well into the future (Quinn, 2015). The Small Business Technology Council identified at least eight major concerns as fall-out from AIA (Schmidt, Jacobus, & Glover, 2014).

Over the last few decades, the Kauffman Foundation has become a prominent supporter of entrepreneurship education, research and data collection (http://www.kauffman. org/who-we-are, 2016).[17] It has also worked diligently to develop an entrepreneurship policy separate and distinct from small business. It has largely failed in that endeavor. The Foundation's policy proposals are usually directed at new rather than entrepreneurial business and typically consist of traditional policy measures, such as special tax treatment for investments in new businesses and reduced regulation for entry (Schramm & Litan, 2011), proposals established small-business interests often include in their agendas. Kauffman's principal policy deviation from the small-business norm is labor. The technology industries, much of which is entrepreneurial, demand increases in skilled workers through immigration and Kauffman augments the position by arguing that immigrant skilled workers have a higher propensity to become entrepreneurs than the native population (Stangler & Wiens, 2016); it is generally silent on labor regulation. That appears to be Kauffman's difference between small and entrepreneurial business policy, other than variation in issue emphasis. The slim difference raises a challenge. If a worthwhile policy difference between the two existed, Kauffman with its resources and access to intellect, would surely have established it by now. And, it has not.

The United States has a technology policy, but not an entrepreneurship policy. The reason for the former is obvious. The reason for the second is that entrepreneurship policy is not distinguishable from what passes for small-business policy, at least in the American context.[18] Entrepreneurship remains associated with small business and when it is not, it is associated with technology-oriented firms. However, reasons for lack of an identifiable entrepreneurship policy extends beyond identity. High-grow firms (technology-oriented and not) usually have well-educated and often wealthy principals; policy subsidizing or otherwise helping the privileged is not likely to receive political sympathy. Entrepreneurial firms can fly as well as dive; policy-makers usually shun the prospect of spectacular loses at public expense. Even new starts as entrepreneurship policy struggles to find support as its principal constituency is not yet born. Beyond money and advice (shelter and support activities), government can do little distinctive to promote high-growth business. For example, it cannot reduce impediments for them without reducing impediments for everyone. That simply puts entrepreneurial firms back under the small-business umbrella. The same is true of taxation. At its heart, entrepreneurship policy is about picking winners and losers (industrial policy); governments have never been good at picking winners and there is little prospect it will improve. The Obama Administration dabbled in industrial policy to an extent not seen since the Depression. However, once the Great Recession subsided and a few politically favored businesses collapsed, public attitudes changed. The likelihood of a separate and distinct entrepreneurship policy, even if definable and desirable, remains bleak.

The quest for political influence

Satagaj divides small-business influence in Washington over the last several decades into three stages – the rise, the apogee, and the decline (J. Satagaj, personal communication, March 19, 2016). He dates the stages roughly as 1976–1985, 1986–2000, and 2001 forward, although the date dividing the second and third stages depends on whether the separation pertains to the Congress or the White House. Regardless, the change in small business's ability to affect policy in Washington grew enormously for several years, eventually rising to its inclusion among Washington's power elite. Motley relates that in the mid-1970s as a lobbyist for the largest small-business organization in the country, he could not obtain an appointment with senior members of Congress to discuss small-business issues (J. Motley, personal communication, March 28, 2016). One-quarter century later, Fortune magazine's Power 25 ranked the NFIB, Motley's organization, the 3rd most powerful lobby in Washington (Birnbaum, 1998).[19]

The ascendancy of small business's influence received an enormous boost from the *Job generation process*. Policy-makers may not have known much about small business, but they did know small business created jobs. Small business also benefited from a cooperating cadre of small business advocates in and out of government, and among both parties, who were dedicated to promoting small business and bringing it center-stage. That level of cooperation reached its apex in the late 1970s and early 1980s and has rarely been seen since. Greater involvement in electoral politics, like the rest of the big boys, also contributed (J. Motley, personal communication, March 28, 2016). Electoral politics implied candidate endorsements, campaign contributions, etc. Direct campaign involvement was not universally accepted across the spectrum of small-business organizations, but it grew among those that did. One clear indicator of rising influence appeared in the development of coalition politics. Organizations and individual businesses, sometimes very diverse ideologically, in size and influence, and political interests, would form ad hoc coalitions to support or oppose a specific policy or policy proposal. Coalitions were fluid. Your friend in the morning's coalition meeting may have been vilified at the afternoon's different coalition meeting. Small-business organizations and trade groups dominated by small firms were particularly attractive coalition members. They put a positive face on the group, and its specific interest could be used to lobby for the coalition's greater effort. Advocates periodically worried that large firms and less transparent interests would try to use them as fronts (J. Satagaj, personal communication, March 19, 2016). Regardless, groups with no influence were not sought out for membership. The small-business problem was not a lack of invitations; it was an excess of them.

The high point

The central event marking small business's political rise was the 1994 defeat of the Clinton national healthcare proposal, sometimes known as Hillarycare, after the President's wife who was charged with developing and promoting the proposal. Passage of the national health insurance plan initially appeared a foregone conclusion. Even corporate business interests, including the U.S. Chamber of Commerce, were ready to buy-in (Judis, 1995). But small-business owners objected and so a few small-business interests ventured out on their own to oppose it. The primary issue to which small business objected in the Clinton healthcare proposal was the same one that it opposed in the Affordable Care Act nearly two decades later – mandatory employer provision and payment of employee health insurance. An intense struggle took place for over a year in which small business prominently participated. In the end, the proposal did not even reach a final vote. Small business emerged newly empowered. A widely read weekly news magazine assessed the political fall-out this way:

> ... NFIB's role in the demise of Clinton's sweeping overhaul plan marks a major shift in Washington's – and the nation's – political culture. No longer do lobbyists for corporate titans ... call the shots for conservatives on big economic issues. The era of grass-roots-oriented lobbying has emerged from the rubble of health care reform. (Headden, 1994)

It was a new day. Successes in the following years were primarily defensive in nature. They were typically measured by what did not happen – what was not debated. Positive accomplishments did occur with the Small Business Regulatory Enforcement Fairness Act (SBREFA), the Bush tax cuts, and the JOBS Act of 2012 as examples. Still, ominous signs began to develop.

Entry costs to grass-roots politics are relatively low once someone has a good, computerized list of like-minded people. NFIB developed the process for small business in the late 1970s; it was highly innovative. Twenty years later everyone could and did use the same process; the one-time political advantage disappeared. A "tired" factor also began to affect small-business influence adversely. It was no longer the new kid on the block; it had engaged in numerous bruising political battles and had come away scarred; once, it had many friends and few enemies – now it had many friends and lots of enemies. New research muddied the shiny portrait of small-business job generation. But far more important than the three reasons just identified were political developments in the larger body politic over which small-business owners had little influence as a group, but may (or may not) have had as individuals. The most prominent was the growing ideological-orientation of the two major political parties.

The early 1980s found moderate to conservative members in the Democrat party and moderate to liberal members in the Republican party. Small business was able to work easily with both sides of the aisle, encouraging bi-partisan activity to pursue its interests. As conservative members evaporated among Democrats, liberals evaporated among Republicans, and moderates simply evaporated, small business found it increasingly difficult to conduct business. Moderates and conservatives had always been more likely to support the evolving small-business agenda regardless of the party to which they belonged.[20] With moderates vanishing and conservatives increasingly lodged in the Republican party, small-business was pigeon-holed as a part of the Republican coalition because both economic agendas tended to be non-interventionist. Democrats thought they had little to gain by supporting small business, at least as it was represented (Kazee, Lipsky, & Martin, 2008). The more organized small business became politically involved, the greater the split, severely depressing its capacity to influence government's direction. By the turn of the century, small business could achieve relatively little unless both sides agreed.

The inability to debate

A major, largely unrecognized problem existed as small business usually lacked adequate quantitative information to defend itself, let alone promote new issue areas. The *Job generation process* filled that gap for a lengthy period. However, the statistical agencies of government offered little help. Counts of enterprises by size of business were only available once every five years in the late 1970s, and even then counts by employee size, industry and geography could not be obtained. Other statistics by size of firm were virtually non-existent and largely remain that way to the present. Small business was left to its own devices to provide the data necessary to make a persuasive argument.

At first, small business presented its case by offering opinions. Organization membership opinion surveys were the staple. Opinion grew thin however, particularly as the agenda shift pushed small-business interests up against other powerful groups with the resources to provide real data and serious studies. The next step was surveys with nationally representative samples emphasizing behavior rather than opinion. SBA's Office of Advocacy stepped in to encourage Census to provide more and better small-business statistics; it also sponsored a small economic research program that yielded some important work (for example, Hopkins, 1995). NFIB, in conjunction with Regional Economic Models Inc., created a modeling system, the only one of its kind, which provided firm size impacts (http://www.nfib.com/foundations/research-foundation/additional-resources/about-the-foundation/, 2016). The organization even ventured into experimental economics with a health care study conducted by a group headed by a Nobel prize winner (Rassenti & Johnston, 2009). Yet, even as the quality and amount of information on small business grew, small business was never able to focus sufficient resources, intellectual and financial, to provide the arguments necessary to adequately debate the current agenda, let alone open new areas of interest.

Given the rise and ebb of small business's political influence and the highly partisan and ideological bent of the present environment, the question becomes whether its influence can be recaptured. Does the current condition represent an interruption in the evolution of increasing sway, or does it represent a new, evolutionary direction? The probable answer is that small business cannot recapture its former political stature, at least until government is united under Republican auspices for an extended duration, the policy agenda returns to support and shelter, or the number of new businesses wanes to the point that it becomes a politically agreed upon national crisis. But failure to recapture the apex does not return it to the base. Small business has become an important political actor and will likely continue to be. Its impact on the economy, individual opportunity, and American self-identity is too great for anything else.

Conclusion

The United States has no small-business policy. There are support and shelter efforts; there are impediment reduction initiatives. But there is no policy in the sense of a conscious strategy that presents a range of activities directed toward small business and then arranges and prioritizes them in some coherent fashion (Storey, 1994). All is ad hoc. That does not imply the evolution of public activities to help small business was directionless. It was, drawing from core American values and changing circumstance to redefine problems and seek (new) solutions (Anglund, 2000). Small business presented new solutions within a new agenda and engaged in a new politics to support it. The *Job generation process* accelerated and intensified the process because it created an empirically based justification for small business to move in its chosen direction.

Washington did make attempts to accommodate small business's new and increasing demands. The process was messy. The new demands presented by small business often came at the expense of other powerful groups, forcing small-business interests to grow up quickly. They did. But new circumstances arose and continue to arise that will likely redirect the course of small-business policy, writ large, from the one it has been following for the last 40–50 years. Divided politics is the most immediate of these circumstances. The Herculean partisan gap in American politics isolates small business, reducing political influence which in turn lessens its ability to impact enactment of its agenda. Moreover, the partisan divide has no foreseeable end. The current political instability necessitates an eventual resolution. How that resolution will affect small business and its agenda is not obvious.

Small-business influence is also likely to be affected by the results of recent economic research. The new emphasis on segments of the small-business population, such as young businesses, (Haltiwanger et al., 2010) splinters the small-business umbrella. The alarming research showing an extended decline in new starts (Haltiwanger et al., 2012) further removes the focus from small business per se and places it on distinct slices of the population. This rupture is not necessarily bad for small business, at least certain segments of it, because policy is more likely to be more informed and the response more appropriate. Yet, when policy targets slices of the population, it tends to be of the support and shelter variety. That focus is not likely to be a good thing for small business generally.

One prominent splinter is likely to occur from the failure to understand that technology business is not equated to entrepreneurial business, and vice versa. The two are typically associated and often have common interests. Technology issues, for the most part absent from the small-business agenda, have grown increasingly prominent as their implications for the entire body politic have become better understood. But non-technology entrepreneurial business shares growth issues with technology entrepreneurially oriented business, but not its industry-specific concerns. These splits are likely to play into the hands of divided politics with technology-based businesses, particularly when they are entrepreneurial, more likely to associate with the Democrat party and more traditional small business with Republican party. These associations are tied to the former's propensity to support government intervention and the latter's to do the opposite, as well as their differing labor requirements. The likely champion of non-technology entrepreneurial business will be dependent on the varying needs of specific business.

New problems and new circumstances create new agendas as well as lift (and lower) interests and individuals that promote (and oppose) them. The United States now seems at a point where new problems and new circumstances seem to be evolving more rapidly and disruptively. Small business will not be immune.

Notes

1. Small business has always enjoyed considerable public regard in the United States. Early in the nation's history, Alexis De Tocqueville noted during his travels an American proclivity to

engage in small commercial ventures (de Tocqueville, 1843). For years, the Gallup Organiz-ation did not even list small business in its annual poll of American institutions' popularity. Small business's inclusion made no sense given its historic high regard. Now included, small business consistently places second on the long list, only behind the military, with two-thirds having confidence in it. By contrast, 42% have confidence ("a great deal" or "quite a lot") in churches or organized religion, 32% in the U.S. Supreme Court, and 21% in big business (Jones, 2015).

2. Elsewhere, the author has argued that public policies affecting small business fall in two cat-egories, one support and other impediment reduction. Effectively, the former is an attempt to help small business hurdle competitive/government imposed barriers to success (however defined) while the latter attempts to tear down those barriers (Dennis, 2015).

3. The three White House Conferences on Small Business held between 1980 and 1995 all selected delegates in a similar manner. The process essentially involved publicized regional and state meetings open to all small-business owners at which policy issues impacting their firms were discussed/debated. These local participants in turn selected delegates to the national conference in Washington. Each conference produced 60 recommendations. The first two also published a top 15 list based on delegate votes. The 1995 Conference refused to produce a top 15 list for political reasons, but the published vote count allowed any observer to create such a tally. A paid Washington-based staff provided more and less sophisticated issue briefing papers for the delegates, and selected overall break-out issue areas for the discussion, such as capital formation or international trade. As many as 50,000 participated in the first two conferences alone. Staff had little control over delegates' decisions and priorities.

4. Full disclosure: The author was employed by the NFIB Research Foundation, an affiliate of the largest small business association in the United States, for 38 years and directed all but two of the surveys in the series. The latest edition was produced by Holly Wade as *Small business problems and priorities*. See Table 5, beginning on page 24 for comparison of relative problem importance over time (Wade, 2012). Representativeness is always an issue in an association survey regardless of the organization's size, and NFIB is a very large one. The NFIB Research Foundation attempted to determine any discrepancies in views held among NFIB members and broader public of small-business owners. Results showed the two populations having similar views on virtually all policy issues (Dennis, 2009a).

5. The House Ways and Means Committee is traditionally regarded as the most powerful and prestigious in the U.S. House of Representatives.

6. Robinson–Patman Act was intended to protect small retailers from discriminatory pricing (use of loss-leaders) by large chain stores and leveraging their market power to force small suppliers, typically manufacturers, to lower their prices.

7. In the mid-1970s, small retailers constituted one-third of all employing small businesses. The figure today stands closer to 10%.

8. John Satagaj was former Legislation Counsel for the SBLC from 1985 through his retirement in 2014. Mr Satagaj also produced the original draft of the Regulatory Flexibility Act of 1980.

9. Internally generated funds, pre-tax profits, is the major source of small business finance. In that context, taxes become a primary small business finance issue. However, taxes typically are placed in a category of their own.

10. The downside of deregulation was the dwindling number of small banks, which are signifi-cantly more small-business friendly than their larger counter-parts. The impact of bank rere-gulation [Dodd–Frank Wall Street Reform and Consumer Act of 2011] on small business lending has yet to be evaluated, though early appearances are not positive.

11. The Act established a process when a projected Federal rule was likely to create a "significant impact" on a "substantial number" of small entities. When that occurred, the agency making the rule had to consider alternatives to reduce the burden for small entities without violating the objectives of the rule-making, and implement them where possible. The Office of Advo-cacy at the Small Business Administration would supervise its implementation.

12. Estimated savings for the years FY 2002 to FY 2006, for example, amounted to $79 billion or about $16 billion annually.
13. The comment refers exclusively to the small business exemption, not to the remainder of the Act which was anything but.
14. Jean-Baptiste Colbert, Louis XIV'S Finance Minister, famously asserted that "the art of taxation consists in so plucking the goose as to obtain the largest possible amount of feathers with the smallest possible amount of hissing". This principle first enunciated in the seventeenth century proved highly effective in the twenty-first.
15. The 50-employee level is actually not as straightforward as it seems. There are issues involving the count of part-time employees and employees in multiple businesses owned by one employer or, more likely, employer group(s). The latter situation is resolved by "aggregation rules" that no more than a handful of people in the country actually understand.
16. Congress created the SBIC program in 1958 to facilitate the flow of long-term capital to America's small businesses. SBA partners with private investors to capitalize professionally managed investment funds (known as "SBICs") that finance small businesses. https://www.sba.gov/sbic. Accessed 18 March 2016.
17. Established in the mid-1960s by the late entrepreneur and philanthropist Ewing Marion Kauffman, the Kauffman Foundation is based in Kansas City, Mo., and is among the largest private foundations in the United States with an asset base of approximately $2 billion. A primary focus of the Foundation is on entrepreneurship. http://www.kauffman.org/who-we-are. Accessed 12 October 2016.
18. Lundström and Stevenson (2010) have made a concerted effort to divorce two entrepreneurship policy and small-business policy, principally by defining entrepreneurship as business starts. Policies that impact pre-starts, starts, and recent post-start are entrepreneurship policies and the remainder of policies impacting smaller firms is small business policy. The authors have conceptually achieved some success, but pragmatically policy-makers have neither the unlimited time frame nor the capacity to develop the coordinated individual activities that their entrepreneurship policy requires.
19. The two organizations ranked higher than NFIB that year were the AARP (American Association of Retired Persons) and AIPAC (American Israel Public Affairs Committee). The rankings in the late 1990s and first few years of the 2000s showed variation with NFIB ranking between second and fourth.
20. The small business agenda in the United States is economic in nature. It does not include social issues or foreign policy. As one noted small business lobbyist was fond of saying, "We don't do busing, abortion, or gun control."

Disclosure statement

No potential conflict of interest was reported by the author.

References

Anglund, S. (2000). *Small business policy and the American creed*. Westport, CT: Praeger.
Bauer, J., & Kintner, E. (1986). The Robinson–Patman Act: A look backwards, a view forward. *Antitrust Bulletin, 31*(Fall), 571–609.
Birch, D. (1979). *Job generation process*. Cambridge: MIT Program on Neighborhood and Regional Change.
Birch, D. (1987). *Job creation in America*. New York, NY: Free Press.
Birnbaum, J. (1998, December 7). The influence merchants. *Fortune*, 134–152.
Board of Governors of the Federal Reserve System. (2007). *Report to the Congress on the availability of credit to small business*. Washington, DC.
Brock, W., & Evans, D. (1985). The economics of regulatory tiering. *Rand Journal of Economics, 16*(3), 398–409.

Brock, W., & Evans, D. (1986). *The economics of small businesses: Their role and regulation in the U.S. economy.* New York, NY: Holmes & Meier.

Butler, S. (1981). *Enterprise zones: Greenlining the inner cities.* New York, NY: Universe Books.

Carpenter, S., & Rowe, K. (2005). The "SOX" effect on small companies: An interview with Paul Vallone of Montgomery & Co. 5 *U.C. Davis Bus. L.J.* 19.

Dennis, W., Jr. (1993). *A small business primer.* Washington, DC: National Federation of Independent Business.

Dennis, W., Jr. (2008). *Small business access to credit: Yesterday, today and tomorrow.* Orebro, Sweden: Swedish Entrepreneurship Forum. Retrieved March 10, 2016, from http://www.entreprenorskapsforum.se/wp-content/uploads/2013/03/WP-01.pdf

Dennis, W., Jr. (2009a). *Opinions of NFIB member & the small business population: Is there a difference?* Washington, DC: National Federation of Independent Business. Retrieved February 25, 2016, from http://www.nfib.com/Portals/0/PDF/AllUsers/research/Opinions%20of%20NFIB%20Members%20and%20the%20Small%20Business%20Population.pdf

Dennis, W., Jr. (2009b). Tailoring regulation to the regulated: The U.S. Regulatory Flexibility Act. In A. Nijsen, J. Hudson, C. Muller, K. van Paridon, & R. Turik (Eds.), *Business regulation and public policy* (pp. 83–95). New York, NY: Springer.

Dennis, W., Jr. (2012). *Small business, credit access, and a lingering recession.* Washington, DC: National Federation of Independent Business. Retrieved March 2016, from http://www.nfib.com/Portals/0/PDF/AllUsers/research/studies/small-business-credit-study-nfib-2012.pdf

Dennis, W., Jr. (2015). Public policy for American small business: Promoting supports and reducing impediments. In S. Newbert (Ed.), *Small business in a global economy* (Vol. 2, pp. 323–348). Santa Barbara, CA: Praeger.

Dunkelberg, W., & Wade, H. (series). *Small business economic trends.* Washington, DC: NFIB Research Foundation.

Emanuel, E., & Fuchs, V. (2008). Who really pays for health care? The myth of "shared responsibility". *The Journal of the American Medical Association, 299*(9), 1057–1059.

Federal Reserve Banks of New York, Atlanta, Cleveland and Philadelphia. (2014). *Joint small business credit survey report, 2014.* New York, NY: Federal Reserve Bank. Retrieved March 10, 2016, from https://www.newyorkfed.org/medialibrary/media/smallbusiness/SBCS-2014-Report.pdf

Guenther, G. (2015). *The Section 179 and bonus depreciation expensing allowances: Current law and issues for the 114th Congress (RL31852).* Washington, DC: Congressional Research Service.

Haltiwanger, J., Jarmin, R., & Miranda, J. (2010). *Who creates job? Small vs. large vs. young* (Working Paper No. 16300). Cambridge, MA: National Bureau of Economic Research.

Haltiwanger, J., Jarmin, R., & Miranda, J. (2012). *Business dynamics statistics briefing: Where have all the young firms gone?* Kansas City, MO: Kauffman Foundation.

Headden, S. (1994, September 12). *The little lobby that could: How small business advocates whipped Clinton on the health care bill.* U.S. News & World Report. pp. 45–48.

Hopkins, T. (1995). *A survey of regulatory burdens* (Contract Number SBA-8029-OA-93). Washington, DC: Office of Advocacy, U.S. Small Business Administration.

Jones, J. (2015). *Confidence in U.S. institutions still below historical norms.* Retrieved February 12, 2016, from http://www.gallup.com/poll/183593/confidence-institutions-below-historical-norms.aspx

Judis, J. (1995, Spring). Abandoned surgery: Business and the failure of health reform. *The American Prospect.* Retrieved March 14, 2016, from http://prospect.org/article/abandoned-surgery-business-andfailure-health-reform

Kaiser Family Foundation, & Health Research & Educational Trust. (2015). *Employer health benefits: 2015 annual survey.* Washington, DC. Retrieved February 15, 2016, from http://files.kff.org/attachment/report-2015-employer-health-benefits-survey

Kazee, N., Lipsky, M., & Martin, C. (2008, July/August). Outside the big box. Who speaks for small business? *Boston Review.* Retrieved March 14, 2016, from http://new.bostonreview.net/archives/BR33.4/kazee.php

Kolasky, W. (2004). What is competition? A comparison of U.S. and European perspectives. *Antitrust Bulletin, 49*(Spring), 29–53.

Lerner, J. (2013). General counsel, Federal Trade Commission letter to the District of Columbia Taxicab Commission, June. Retrieved March 10, 2016, from https://www.ftc.gov/sites/default/files/documents/advocacy_documents/ftc-staff-comments-district-columbia-taxicab-commission-concerning-proposed-rulemakings-passenger/130612dctaxicab.pdf

Lerner, J., Speen, A., & Leamon, A. (2015). *Leahy-Smith American invents Act: A preliminary examination of its impact on small businesses* (Contract Number SBAHQ-14-Q-0011). Washington, DC: Office of Advocacy, Small Business Administration.

Lundström, A., & Stevenson, L. (2010). *Entrepreneurship policy: Theory and practice.* New York, NY: Springer.

Macrae, N. (1976, December). The new entrepreneurial revolution. *The Economist,* pp. 42–45.

Mattappally, J. (2012). Goliath beats David: Undoing the Leahy-Smith Americans Invent Act's harmful effects on small businesses. *Loyola Law Review, 58*(4), 981–1034. Retrieved April 9, 2016, from http://law.loyno.edu/law-review-volume-58-number-4

Mills, C., & McCarthy, B. (2014). *The state of small business lending: Credit access during the recovery and how technology may change the game* (Working Paper 15-004). Cambridge, MA: Harvard Business School. Retrieved from http://www.hbs.edu/faculty/Publication%20Files/15-004_09b1bf8b-eb2a-4e63-9c4e-0374f770856f.pdf Accessed March 10, 2016

National Small Business Association. (2014). *2014 politics of small business.* Washington, DC. Retrieved March 20, 2016, from http://nsba.biz/docs/Politics-Survey-2014.pdf

Office of Advocacy, US Small Business Administration. (2016). *Report on the Regulatory Flexibility Act, FY 2015.* Washington, DC: Office of Advocacy, U.S. Small Business Administration. Retrieved March 14, 2016, from https://www.sba.gov/sites/default/files/advocacy/FY_15_RFA_Report_newTC_pp1-72.pdf

Quinn, G. (2015, May 7). *Patent reform 101 – A primer on pending patent legislation.* Retrieved April 9, 2016, from http://www.ipwatchdog.com/2015/05/07/patent-reform-101-a-primer-on-pending-patent-legislation/id=57529/

Rassenti, S., & Johnston, C. (2009). *Health insurance reform in an experimental market.* Washington, DC: NFIB Research Foundation.

Schmidt, R., Jacobus, H., & Glover, J. (2014). *Why 'patent reform' harms innovative small businesses.* Retrieved April 9, 2016, from http://www.ipwatchdog.com/2014/04/25/why-patent-reform-harms-innovative-small-businesses/id=49260/

Schramm, C., & Litan, R. (2011). The startup act: A proposal to jumpstart the economy. *Huffington Post.* Retrieved April 9, 2016, from http://www.huffingtonpost.com/carl-j-schramm/the-startup-act-a-proposa_b_902360.html

Scott, J., & Dunkelberg, W. (2005). *Evaluating banks, national small business poll* (Vol. 5, Issue 7). Washington, DC: NFIB Research Foundation. Retrieved March 10, 2016, from http://www.411sbfacts.com/sbpoll.php?POLLID=0049

Stangler, D., & Wiens, J. (2016). The case for welcoming immigrant entrepreneurs. *Entrepreneurship Policy Digest.* Retrieved September 15, 2016, from http://www.kauffman.org/what-we-do/resources/entrepreneurship-policy-digest/the-economic-case-for-welcoming-immigrant-entrepreneurs

Storey, D. (1994). *Understanding the small business sector.* London, UK: Routledge.

Summers, L. (1989). Some simple economics of mandated benefits. *The American Economic Review, 79*(2), 177–183.

de Tocqueville, A. (1843). *Democracy in America.* In P. Bradley (Ed.) (1972). New York, NY: Alfred A. Knopf.

U.S. Congress Joint Committee on Taxation. (2015). *Present law and legislative background relating to depreciation and Section 179 expensing* (JCX 54-05). Washington, DC.

U.S. House of Representatives, Committee on Ways and Means. (2009). *Hearing: Health reform in the 21st century: Employer–sponsored insurance* (Serial 111–17).

U.S. Regulatory Council. (1981). *Tiering regulations: A practical guide.* Washington, DC: The White House.

Wade, H. (2012). *Small business problems and priorities.* Washington, DC: NFIB Research Foundation. Retrieved February 25, 2016, from https://www.nfib.com/Portals/0/PDF/AllUsers/research/studies/small-business-problems-priorities-2012-nfib.pdf

White House Commission on Small Business. (1980). *America's small business economy: Agenda for action: Report to the president*. Washington, DC: US Government Printing Office. Retrieved February 25, 2016, from http://babel.hathitrust.org/cgi/pt?id=mdp.39015019046534;view=1up; seq=56

White House Commission on Small Business. (1986). *America's small business economy: Agenda for action: Report to the president*. Washington, DC: US Government Printing Office. Retrieved February 25, 2016, from http://babel.hathitrust.org/cgi/pt?id=mdp.39015019046534;view=1up; seq=36

White House Commission on Small Business. (1996). *America's small business economy: Agenda for action: Report to the president*. Washington, DC: US Government Printing Office. Retrieved February 25, 2016, from https://www.sba.gov/sites/default/files/files/stateofsb1996.pdf

The evolution of small business policy in Australia and New Zealand

Tim Mazzarol and Delwyn Clark

ABSTRACT
The paper outlines the evolution of small business policy in Australia and New Zealand. Adopting an historical perspective, changes in policies and programs from the 1970s to the present for these two nations are discussed and compared. Starting with an overview of the nature of small business policy and its emergence internationally, the distinction between small business policy and entrepreneurship policy is considered. Details of the major policy developments for each country are presented by decade, linked to their national governments and the core policy fields. Both countries follow similar patterns of increasing policy sophistication and the transition from small business to entrepreneurship policy. Similarities are most likely due to their closer economic and social ties, and the tendency to look at international trends and adopt them. Australia has retained significant focus on small-to-medium enterprises, whereas New Zealand has moved towards entrepreneurial firms and the enabling environment for all businesses.

Introduction

This article examines the evolution of small business policy in Australia and New Zealand. Its focus is on the emergence of small business and entrepreneurship as a specific area of policy development within these national governments from the 1970s to the present. However, it also seeks to place the emergence of small business policy in these two nations into a wider context associated with similar developments in other countries. Specifically, it examines the transition of small business policy as one that has shifted from "small business policy" (SBP) to "entrepreneurship policy" (EP) (Lundström et al., 2014).

This transition from an SBP centric to an EP-centric policy focus is a trend found in many other countries (United Nations Conference on Trade and Development [UNCTAD], 2012). It reflects a desire within governments to use the small firms sector as an engine room of economic and employment growth. Although this desire for growth is to be expected from governments facing economic downturns and rising unemployment, the reality is that most small-to-medium enterprises (SMEs) are not interested in growth, particularly high growth (Nightingale & Coad, 2014). Much of the net new employment that is created is due to a few high-growth "Gazelle" firms that are estimated to comprise, on average, less than 1% of all firms by employment, or 2% by turnover (Organisation for Economic Co-operation and Development [OECD], 2010a). However, due to their rapid growth, such firms are inherently very risky. The investment into EP and the generation of "Gazelle" start-ups are now being challenged by research suggesting that it may be doing little to generate employment (Acs, Astebro, Audretsch, & Robinson, 2016; Davila, Foster, He, & Shimizu, 2015). Some entrepreneurship scholars have suggested that public funding focusing on high-growth start-ups would be better spent on areas such as education and healthcare (Shane, 2009).

This article begins with an overview of the nature of small business policy, what it comprises and its general emergence at an international level. It then examines the historical evolution of small business policy in Australia and New Zealand by comparing the changes that have been made over time in the two countries and the forces that have shaped them. The policy developments that have evolved are also considered in terms of a series of six core policy areas. Finally, future directions for small business policy and recommendations on areas that could be given more attention are discussed. This includes suggestions for both policy-makers seeking to develop future small business policies in these two countries, and academic researchers who wish to explore this largely ignored area of small business research.

The nature of small business policy

Although there is no universally accepted definition of an SME, one of the most commonly used definitions is that of the European Commission. This defines an SME as an autonomous business with less than 250 employees, an annual turnover below €50 million and with assets of less than €43 million (OECD, 2004). Bennett (2014) suggests that small business policy is a significant activity across many countries because in most economies SMEs comprise the majority of all businesses. This was highlighted in a survey of 40 developed economies that found SMEs comprised around 99% of all businesses in those countries (OECD, 2010b). Policies differ across nations and reflect the social, political and economic conditions within each country. However, most small business and entrepreneurship policy focuses around on at least six primary policy fields illustrated in Figure 1. These include: (i) creation of a business enabling environment; (ii) providing business development services; (iii) providing debt and equity financing; (iv) fostering an entrepreneurial culture; (v) facilitating the diffusion of innovation and technology and (vi) ensuring market access (Bennett, 2014).

The first of these deals with legal and regulatory frameworks that enhance the ability of SMEs to get started, grow and survive. It also encompasses the physical infrastructure such as the transport, communications, power, water and other public works that facilitate business. This can also include the provision of business incubators and industrial estates. The second field deals with the provision of professional and advisory services for SMEs. The third field is associated with the provision of financing for SMEs across all stages of the lifecycle and is closely linked to the banking and financial services sector. The fourth field relates to policies that seek to foster entrepreneurship through education and training, business incubation, support and public awareness. The fifth field

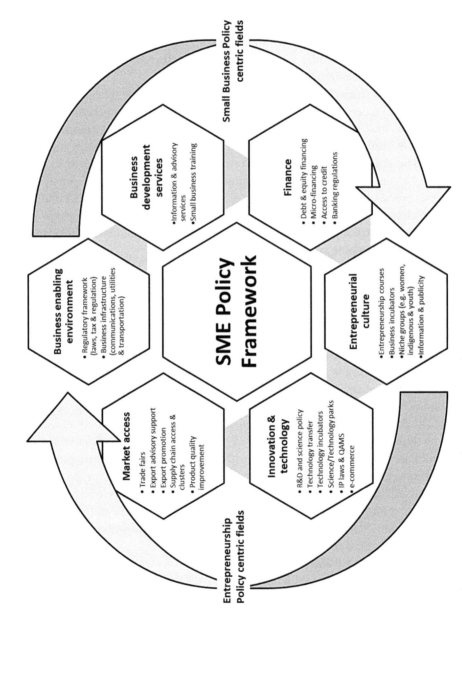

Figure 1. SME policy framework. Source: adapted from Bennett (2014).

encompasses a range of issues such as intellectual property (IP) laws and technology transfer from universities. Finally, the sixth field focuses on programs designed to assist SMEs with export and access to government and industry supply chains. As illustrated in Figure 1, the first three are primarily SBP centric while the last three are primarily EP centric.

From SBP to EP

Small business, as a specific area of policy focus within government, is a phenomenon that has emerged strongly since at least the 1970s. However, its antecedents can be traced back to the late nineteenth century. For example, Blackford (2003), in his analysis of the history of small business in the United States, points to the period between 1880 and 1920 when big corporations became particularly dominant in America. This placed at risk the viability of their small business counterparts. In response government policies emerged that were designed to address market power and distortions, with a focus on anti-trust and associational activity by corporations. A similar pattern of activity took place in Germany, where the emergence of large corporations and monopolies during the period from the 1850s to the 1920s created significant pressure on the SME sector or *Mittelstand*. It led many economists and political parties to suggest that the predictions of Marx and Engels over the destruction of all small businesses (*kleine Mittelstände*) by the rise of big corporations would eventually become a reality (Berghoff, 2006).

The rise of organised labour trade unions and their associated political parties in the late nineteenth century was a response to the increasing power of the large corporations. Both unions and corporations used their influence to shape policy within government. However, this left the small business owners and skilled artisans caught in the middle without a strong political voice, apart from what they might get through chambers of commerce or industry associations (Blackbourn, 1977). Throughout the twentieth century, the political importance of small business owners and farmers was acknowledged by politicians, particularly those on the right, who sought to secure their support against the political parties that represented the trade unions (Blackford, 2003; Von Saldern, 1992). The small business community became associated with a "middle" that fell between big corporations and big unions.

In the United States the cycle of two world wars and the 1930s Great Depression led to strong calls within political circles to recognise the importance of the small business community. This resulted in the passage of the Small Business Act of 1953, and the subsequent establishment of the Small Business Administration (SBA) (Bean, 2000). Within America, small business became associated with freedom, individualism, equality of opportunity and even democracy itself (Anglund, 2000). By comparison, in Germany the *Mittelstand*, which had initially supported the conservative political parties (including the Nazi Party) in the 1930s, emerged from the chaos of the Second World War to become a key part of the economic recovery of that country (Berghoff, 2006; Simon, 1992). Despite these developments, it was the economic stagnation of the early 1970s that saw the most fundamental shift in government interest in small business policy (Blackburn & Schaper, 2012, p. 5).

An indicator of this trend was Britain's 1971 Committee of Inquiry into Small Firms commonly known as the Bolton Report (Bolton, 1971). This provided an in-depth analysis of the nature of small business, its definition and contribution to the economy of the United Kingdom (UK). The report made over 60 recommendations for government policy to address the specific needs of small business. The contribution of SMEs to job creation was also noted. However, Bolton (1982) notes that the inquiry found a "sublime state of indifference" within government and the broader community to the small business sector in the UK. By the end of the decade the Wilson Committee Review of 1979 examined the functioning of the UK's financial institutions and their financing of small firms. This produced a total of 15 recommendations that broadly supported those of the earlier Bolton Report (Bolton, 1971, 1982).

Another major development in America was the publication of Birch's (1979) report *The Job Generation Process*, into the role of small firms in the creation of new jobs in the United States. Although criticised for flaws in its methodology and lack of theoretical foundation (see Tuerck, Ahiakpor, Fitzroy, Latona, & Foray, 1990), the study sparked renewed interest by governments around the world in small business policy as a solution to high unemployment (Landström, 2005). It was promoted in the media and this helped to foster a range of policies targeting small business start-ups with an emphasis on young high-growth firms known as "Gazelles", which were thought to be the key generators of new employment (Birch, 1987). The emergence of small business as a major policy issue also spread throughout the world during this period (Blackburn & Schaper, 2012). Even China witnessed a transition with the appointment in 1978 of Deng Xiaoping as leader of the Chinese Community Party (CCP). From 1949 until that time, all private businesses in China were taken under state-ownership. However, the rise of Deng led to a policy of economic liberalisation and the official recognition of Township and Village Enterprises and later SMEs (Ye, Tweed, & Toulson, 2012).

From these early beginnings in the 1970s and 1980s the formalisation of small business policy grew at a global level, as reflected in the creation of government agencies and ministerial portfolios dedicated to this area. Over the period from the 1990s to the present, SBP became supplemented by EP. The differences between these two areas are fuzzy and there are many overlaps. However, Lundström et al. (2014) suggest that EP can be defined as those policy measures targeted at start-up or early stage ventures (usually the first 3 years). By comparison SBP should be defined as policies aimed at established firms (over 3 years old), with less than 250 employees. EP has also been identified with the four key areas of focus: (i) E-Extension policies, targeted at start-up support services and early stage financing; (ii) new firm creation policy, focused on removing barriers to new firm creation and exit; (iii) "niche" entrepreneurship policy, involving policies designed to increase entrepreneurship amongst specific groups (e.g. women, youth) and (iv) "Holistic" EP, which includes policies that aim to enhance the overall level of entrepreneurial culture, climate and capacity within the society (Lundström & Stevenson, 2010).

EP has also become interwoven with innovation policy in recent years, with the latter having emerged from science and technology policy (OECD, 2006). This has evolved from a technology-driven or "science push" approach in the pre-1990s era, into a market-driven or "demand-led" focus in more recent times (Dahlstrand & Stevenson, 2007). Rigby and Ramlogan (2013) argued that EP and SBP both aim to improve economic outcomes. However, EP is focused on the individual entrepreneur within the business, while SBP is focused on the competitiveness of the business itself. Mason and Brown (2014) suggest that SBP is largely "transactional" in nature (e.g. taxation, subsidies), while EP is "relational" (e.g. network building, mentoring). Bennett (2014) identifies four main fields where government support for entrepreneurs and small firms is focused through policy. The first of these is institutional capacity building (e.g. legislation and regulation). A second area is the reduction of risk for entrepreneurs and small firms via the setting of macroeconomic policy. The third field is associated with cost reduction (e.g. taxation, compliance costs and "red tape"). Finally, there is the flow of information including mentoring, advisor support services, education and training.

Government interest in small business and entrepreneurship policies were initially motivated by recognition that SMEs comprise a significant part of the business community. However, in more recent times the interest has been driven by a belief that entrepreneurship and small business development can provide a "universal cure" to help lower unemployment and boost flagging economic growth (Bridge, 2010). But government's impact on the small business sector, and specifically the behaviour of entrepreneurs, is likely to be more indirect than direct. Macroeconomic policy settings, provision of infrastructure, removal of unnecessary "red tape" regulatory burdens and the application of fair and competitive taxation regimes will more likely provide benefits to SMEs and entrepreneurs than direct intervention and support schemes (Bennett, 2014). Multi-country studies undertaken by the OECD (2010a) support this suggesting an emphasis on enhancing the business environment to assist high-growth strategies by SMEs, fostering entrepreneurship and entrepreneurial cultures via education and training, as well as provision of better access to debt and equity financing, R&D, protection of IP rights and a focus on internationalisation by small business owners. However, the OECD (2010a) also noted that relatively few programs existed across the OECD group of advanced economies, and that the impact and effectiveness of those programs that did exist had not been undertaken.

The small business sector in Australia and New Zealand

Australia and New Zealand share a common history, cultural affinity, geographic proximity and close economic integration under the Australia–New Zealand Closer Economic Relations Trade Agreement (ANZCERTA) (Department of Foreign Affairs and Trade [DFAT], 2016). Both countries are high income developed economies with a combined market of just over 28 million people. Australia is the larger of the two with a population of about 23.5 million people and a land area of more than 7.69 million square kilometres (World Bank, 2016a). By comparison New Zealand has a population of just over 4.5 million and a land area of 265,021 square kilometres (World Bank, 2016b). In both countries, the small business sector comprises a very large proportion of the total stock of businesses. For example, Australia has around 2.5 million actively trading businesses of which less than 1% is large companies (Department of Innovation, Industry, Science and Research [DIISR], 2011). A similar pattern is found in New Zealand where less than 1% of the country's 502,170 businesses are large (Ministry of Business, Innovation and Enterprise [MBIE], 2016).

The Australian Bureau of Statistics (ABS, 2002) defines a small business as an enterprise that is independently owned and operated, under the close control of its owner-managers, who contribute most of the capital and are the principal decision makers. Such firms will be classified as micro-businesses if they employ fewer than 5 people, small businesses if they employ between 5 and 19 people, and medium businesses if they employ between

20 and 199 people. By comparison the New Zealand Ministry of Business Innovation and Employment (MBIE, 2016), which reports that there is no official definition of a small business in New Zealand, notes that some legislation and historical data assume firms with fewer than 20 employees are small, and medium enterprises have between 20 and 50 employees (MBIE, 2016).

In Australia 99.7% of all businesses are SMEs with 95.6% small and 4.1% medium. Non-employing micro-businesses account for 60% of all firms (DIISR, 2011). In New Zealand 99.4% of all firms are SMEs (OECD, 2010b), with 97% of all firms being small with fewer than 20 employees, and only 1% of businesses employing more than 50 employees. Non-employing micro-businesses comprise 70% of all firms (MBIE, 2016). In terms of their impact on employment Australian SMEs account for around 76% of all employment (DIISR, 2011). In New Zealand firms with fewer than 50 employees provide 43% of all jobs (MBIE, 2016), and firms with less than 250 employees around 57.5% of all employment (OECD, 2010b). Overall the SME sector in both nations is a significant part of the national economy, and makes a major contribution to the level of employment and economic growth (DIISR, 2011; MBIE, 2016). However, most SMEs are micro-enterprises with relatively little orientation towards growth, globalisation or innovation (Hendrickson, Bucifal, Balaguer, & Hansell, 2015).

Developing small business policy in Australia and New Zealand

Academic research has given limited attention to the development of small business policy in Australia and New Zealand. However, Jurado and Massey (2012) and Schaper (2014) provide some recent historical overviews of this subject; earlier work in New Zealand includes Nyamori and Lawrence (1997), Massey and Cameron (1999), and Massey and Ingley (2007). The evolution of small business policy in these two countries can be divided into eras that coincide with the period of various governments and the economic cycles that both countries were experiencing. Given the relatively close economic and social relationship between Australia and New Zealand, the trajectory followed by both nations is quite similar.

New Zealand's economic transition 1970 to 2015

The historical timeline for New Zealand is provided in Table 1 which shows that the period from 1970 to 2015 was comprised of an almost continuous rotation of conservative National Party (NP) and social democratic New Zealand Labour Party (NZLP) governments. As a small country, heavily dependent on the export of agricultural commodities, New Zealand is susceptible to global economic downturns. However, high tariff barriers helped to protect local manufacturing and employment, but made the economy less internationally competitive. The late 1960s saw the UK moving towards integration into the European Economic Community (EEC), which it finally did in 1973. The same year saw the OPEC oil crisis that followed the 1973 Yom Kippur War between Israel and its neighbouring Arab states. This impacted New Zealand significantly triggering a serious economic recession, currency devaluation and setting the country on a path to market deregulation (Bordo, Hargreaves, & Kida, 2011). From the late-1970s to the end of the 1990s successive New Zealand governments progressively deregulated the economy and

Table 1. Small business policy development New Zealand 1970–2016.

New Zealand Labour Government (1972–1975)
PM[a] Norman Kirk (1972–1974) and PM Bill Rowling (1974–1975). Focused on state ownership. Acquired Development Finance Corporation (DFC) as state owned enterprise. Economy impacted by UK joining EEC 1973 and the OPEC oil crisis 1973–1974.

National Government (1975–1984)
PM Robert Muldoon began cautious deregulation program. Established NZ Small Business Agency (NZSBA) within DFC to deliver direct assistance to SMEs. But was focused on large firms and industry development via "Think Big" program (1980). Signed the Australia-New Zealand Closer Economic Relations (CER) free trade agreement (1983).

Labour Government (1984–1990)
PM David Lange (1984–1989); PM Geoffrey Palmer (1989–1990); PM Mike Moore (1990). Major economic reforms: floating dollar; financial market deregulation; removal or lowering of tariffs; removal of farm subsidies; lowered company tax; privatised state owned enterprises; introduced goods and services tax (GST). Abolished NZSBA (1987) on grounds that SMEs did not need assistance within a free market.

National Government (1990–1999)
PM Jim Bolger (1990–1997); PM Jenny Shipley (1997–1999). Continued sell-off of state owned enterprises and free market orientation. Major overhaul of employment law that abolished collective bargaining and weakened trade unions. Established Business Development Boards (BDBs) under Ministry of Commerce (later Ministry of Economic Development, MED) (1990) to enable SMEs to contribute to regional development. Delivery of advisory and training programs to help the development of SME competitiveness via management education, growth and exporting. BDBs discontinued (1998). Also, targeted Maori and other minorities into employment via Enterprise Assistance Program (EAP). Shifted focus from low growth SMEs to the few high-growth "Gazelle" firms.

Labour Government (1999–2008)
PM Helen Clark (1999–2008). Continued with economic reforms with intervention in air and rail transport. Promoted "Kiwi Made" local purchasing. Est. Small Business Advisory Group to advise Minister on SME issues and Small Business Directorate within MED (2003), SME Officials Group and Ministerial Group on SMEs. Promoted entrepreneurship amongst Maori and other minorities. Movement from SME policy to entrepreneurship policy focus. "Bright Future" (1999) policy focused on entrepreneurship, innovation and high-growth firms. Focus on high-tech industries and start-ups. Introduced Minister of Small Business (2001) and Growth and Innovation Framework (2002). Est. NZ Trade & Enterprise (NZTE) (2003) to focus on boosting the competitiveness of SMEs and exports, providing Enterprise Awards and managing the BIZ program. Collaboration and public-private partnership programs introduced to develop/increase capabilities.

National Government (2008–present)
PM John Key (2008–present). Came to office following Global Financial Crisis (GFC) 2007–2008. Reduced taxes, increased GST threshold, introduced nine-day working fortnight for employment flexibility, boosted minimum wages and brought in "mixed ownership model" to reduce government shareholdings in many large corporations. Est. Ministry of Business, Innovation and Employment (MBIE) to integrate portfolios for business, science, innovation, education, employment, building, housing energy and tourism, as well as servicing intellectual property, companies' office, insolvency and consumer affairs. Also, runs web-portal www.business.govt.nz Business Growth Agenda (2012) focus on capital markets, innovation, skilled and safe workplaces, resources, infrastructure and export markets. Focus on creating the enabling environment for all business rather than SME-specific policies. Minister of Small Business position retained, SBAG renamed SBDG, and responsibility for SMEs dispersed across various portfolios held by 18 Ministers. Entrepreneurial and high-growth firms prioritised.

[a]Prime Minister (PM).

encouraged free trade. This process was assisted by the signing of the Australia–New Zealand Closer Economic Relations (CER) free trade agreement in 1983, which provided New Zealand companies with easier access to the larger Australian market and opened the New Zealand market for competition with Australian firms. By the end of the twentieth century the New Zealand economy was one of the most globally competitive (Singleton, 2008). The first decade and a half of the current century has seen both NZLP and NP governments pursue free market policies designed to make New Zealand more internationally competitive.

Australia's economic transition 1970 to 2015

Australia's economic history, as outlined in Table 2, followed a similar pattern to New Zealand with both the conservative Liberal National Party (LNP) coalition and the Australian Labor Party (ALP) rotating periods of government throughout the period. Like

Table 2. Small business policy development Australia 1970–2016.

Labor Government (1972–1975)

PM[a] Gough Whitlam (1972–1975). Focus was on social change, higher wages and increased spending on health and education. However, the economy was impacted by UK joining EEC 1973 and the OPEC oil crisis 1973–1974. Stagflation and economic recession made SME policy of low priority. Wiltshire Committee Report (1971) provides first working definition of "small business" and acknowledges the importance of SME sector to economy and need for government policy support. Est. of National Small Business Bureau (NSBB) (1973) to research small business and review legislation impacting SMEs.

Liberal National (Coalition) Government (1975–1983)

PM Malcolm Fraser (1975–1983). Austerity budgeting and rising industrial relations disputes dominated. Limited focus on economic reforms despite stagnant economy. Main focus was on large firms and SMEs were not given significant policy attention. NSBB closed in 1976.

Labor Government (1983–1996)

PM Bob Hawke (1983–1991) and PM Paul Keating (1991–1996). Undertook major economic reforms including floating of currency, deregulation of banks, telecommunications and transport industries, lowering of tariffs and sale of state owned enterprises. Strong focus on industrial relations reforms and "Accord" between large trade unions and big business. Federal funding of New Enterprise Incentive Scheme (NIES) to help unemployed start-up ventures (1986). Appointment of first federal Small Business Minister (Barry Jones) in 1988. Publication of Beddall Report (1990) Parliamentary Inquiry into the challenges, problems and opportunities facing SMEs in Australia. Defined "small business" and made wide range of recommendations for assisting SMEs. Karpin Report (1995) on business competitiveness. Est. AusIndustry (1995) to support business development along with Pooled Development Funds (1992), Co-operative Research Centres (CRCs). At state government level this period saw the emergence of Business Enterprise Centres (BEC) network and Small Business Development Corporations and small business incubators. Encouraged SME growth and export activity.

Liberal National (Coalition) Government (1996–2007)

PM John Howard (1996–2007). Continuation of market deregulation and sale of state-owned enterprises. Introduction of Goods and Services Tax (GST). Strong focus on industrial relations to reduce power of trade unions and increase the level of productivity and employment flexibility. National Productivity Commission established. Est. Department of Workplace Relations and Small Business. Major focus on reduction of "red tape" and removal of unfair dismissal laws, particularly for small firms. Major reviews included Small Business Deregulation Taskforce (1996) and "More Time for Business" (1997) targeted specifically at policies to assist SMEs. Also "Finding a Balance" (1997) that reviewed imbalance between small and large firms in the economy. Est. "R&D Start Program" (1997) and Innovation Investment Fund (IIF) (1997). Introduced Franchising Code of Conduct (1998). Est. Commercialising Emerging Technologies (COMET) grants (2000). Senate review of the "Effectiveness of the Trade Practices Act in Protecting Small Business" (2004). Amended Trade Practices Act (2006). Introduced Independent Contractors' Act (2006), appointed Small Business Commissioner to Australian Competition and Consumer Commission (2008). Small Business Enterprise Program (SBEP) targeted at job creation.

Labor Government (2007–2013)

PM Kevin Rudd (2007–2010); PM Julia Gillard (2010–2013); PM Kevin Rudd (2013). Economy impacted by the Global Financial Crisis (GFC) (2007–2008). Focused on stimulus to the economy. Reviewed Franchising Codes and regulations (2008). Est. Department of Innovation, Industry, Science and Research (DIISR) (2007–2011) putting entrepreneurship and small business policy into one agency. Programs delivered by AusIndustry (e.g. Enterprise Connect) focusing on SME growth in targeted industries. Appointment of first national Small Business Commissioner (2012).

Liberal National (Coalition) Government (2013–2016)

PM Tony Abbott (2013–2015) and PM Malcolm Turnbull (2015–2016). Appointment Small Business Minister (Bruce Billson) to inner cabinet. Strong emphasis on SME policy during era of Billson with creation of the Australian Small Business and Family Enterprise Ombudsman (ASBFEO) Act (2015). Industry Skills Fund (ISF), tax cuts for SMEs.

[a]Prime Minister (PM).

New Zealand, Australia's economy was built on the export of commodities, particularly agricultural produce and minerals, with manufacturing protected behind tariff walls. Government regulation at both federal and state level was high, and industrial relations and wage setting was set by legislative and judicial regulation. Despite enjoying an economic boom in the 1960s, Australia was also hit hard by the OPEC oil crisis of 1973 and the global economic downturn that it generated. Britain's decision to join the EEC also had an impact, but this was lessened by the greater diversification of the Australian economy. Declining global commodity prices forced Australia's governments to commence a process of market deregulation and the opening up of the economy to greater competition. The recession of 1982–1983 saw unemployment rise to around 10% and this led to a period of major economic reform. Economic competitiveness, productivity, industrial relations reform, innovation, enterprise and greater globalisation of industries were all features of the ALP and later LNP governments throughout the 1980s and 1990s. By the end of the twentieth century Australia was ranked amongst the world's most innovative and competitive economies and one of the few to withstand the Global Financial Crisis (GFC) of 2008–2009 with relatively little negative impact (Attard, 2008). During the past decade and a half, all Australian governments have continued this pattern of embracing the free market and global competitiveness through innovation and internationalisation.

Small business policy development in the 1970s

Prior to the 1970s neither Australia nor New Zealand had any formal SBP at the national level. One of the first steps towards the development of SBP in Australia was the establishment of the Wiltshire Committee on Small Business (1971) that had been commissioned during the period of the LNP government of Prime Minister John Gorton (Wiltshire, 1974). It was specifically requested by the Deputy Prime Minister and Minister for Trade and Industry John McEwen, leader of the coalition Country (now National) Party. The Wiltshire Report was the first major government review of the small business sector and laid the foundations for future SBP within Australia. This included a definition of small business, the significance of the sector, the challenges it faced, the need for government support, and how educational institutions could assist with management skills development (Schaper, 2014).

The ALP government of Prime Minister Gough Whitlam that took office in 1972 adopted some of the Wiltshire Report's recommendations, including the establishment of a National Small Business Bureau (NSBB) in Canberra, which opened in 1973. However, it did not adopt other recommendations such as the provision, via private sector and industry associations, of consultancy and support services to SMEs (Landström, 2005). The NSBB pioneered government research into SMEs as well as reviewing legislation and supporting the development of SBP initiatives (Meredith, 1993). However, the NSBB was closed by the LNP government of Prime Minister Malcolm Fraser in 1976. At the state level, New South Wales (NSW) established a Small Business Development Council (SBDC) in 1976 to provide advice to the state government and passed the *Small Businesses' Loans Guarantee Act, 1977*. This provided loan guarantees to financial institutions to assist SMEs seeking finance (Schaper, 2014).

These developments taking place in Australia and elsewhere during the 1970s had an impact on New Zealand, causing policy-makers to take more notice of the SME sector, leading to the establishment in 1978 of the New Zealand Small Business Agency (NZSBA). A branch of the Development Finance Corporation (DFC), the NZSBA was tasked to foster cooperation and coordination between government and non-government organisation to deliver support to SMEs (Devlin & Le Heron, 1977). This period saw SBP in New Zealand running concurrently with regional employment policy due to the major role SMEs play in regional economies. However, the primary focus of the NZLP governments of Prime Ministers Norman Kirk and later Bill Rowling was on state-ownership, while their successor Prime Minister Robert Muldoon's NP government focused primarily on large firms and major industry projects as evidenced by their "Think Big" program of 1980 (Jurado & Massey, 2012).

For both Australia and New Zealand, the 1970s was a period of economic crisis and stagnation accompanied by social and political change. Their closeted and heavily regulated economies were impacted by global economic and political forces that forced their governments to take action that would subsequently see massive market deregulation. There was also little interest shown in either small business or entrepreneurship at the universities, apart from a few pioneers such as Professor Geoffrey Meredith at the University of New England (Gillin, 1991), who had been an advisor to the Wiltshire Committee (Landström, 2005). While the development of SBP remained in its infancy the foundations were laid for its emergence in the decades that followed. Regarding the SME Policy Framework (Figure 1), the 1970s saw little active SBP/EP initiatives other than the emerging recognition of the importance of SMEs and their unique characteristics and problems. Paucity of reliable data on the size, structure and economic contribution of the sector were partly responsible, but so too was the underlying political culture of those times. Government policy was primarily oriented towards what Thurik (2009) describes as a *Schumpeter Mark II regime* or "managed economy". The focus remained on "big business" and "big trade unions" much as it had in the late nineteenth and early twentieth centuries (OECD, 2010b).

Small business policy development in the 1980s

For Australia and New Zealand, the 1980s was a major period of economic reform and the era in which the first evidence of EP-centric policies began to emerge. In New Zealand, the NZLP government of Prime Minister David Lange embarked on a robust and wide-ranging program of economic reform. Jurado and Massey (2012) stated that:

> The underlying government philosophy of this era was that the market should regulate the economy and businesses should operate in a market environment with limited government intervention. (p. 37)

The NZSBA was closed in 1987 because it was considered unnecessary as sufficient support already existed for SMEs via local regional development boards and professional associations. The work of the NZSBA was transferred to the local Business Development Boards (BDBs) that were established in 1990 under the control of the NZ Ministry of Commerce.

In Australia, the ALP governments of Prime Ministers Bob Hawke and Paul Keating also embarked on a major program of economic reform. The sharp recession of 1982–1983 that brought about a change of government and the high unemployment that it created, helped to drive SBP and EP-centric initiatives at both federal and state levels. The New Enterprise Incentive Scheme launched in 1986, provided unemployed people support to start-up their own small business. In 1988 the first federal Minister for Small Business (Barry Jones) was appointed and he commissioned a parliamentary inquiry into the state of the SME sector, which resulted in the Beddall Report of 1990 (Beddall, 1990). This built on the work of the earlier Wiltshire Report, providing a working definition of SMEs and made 66 recommendations across a wide-range of areas. It recognised the problems facing SMEs, the lack of "identity" and definition within the sector and its fragmentation. The need for more coherent and "whole of government" approaches to their support in policy formulation was also acknowledged. Also identified were the needs for better research into SMEs, changes to legislation and regulation, as well as improvements in education and assistance programs (Beddall, 1990).

At the state level, governments also began to embrace SBP. For example, SBDC were established in Queensland in 1980, Western Australia (WA) in 1983, South Australia (SA) in 1984 and NSW in the same year (Schaper, 2014). Business Enterprise Centres (BECs) designed to provide direct support to start-up and established SMEs were first launched in WA in 1987 and rapidly spread. They were influenced by the work of Ernesto Sirolli who pioneered local enterprise facilitation in WA (Sirolli, 2004).

Parallel with this evolution of SBP in Australia, the 1980s also saw the emergence of EP-centric policies. The first "Enterprise Workshop" designed to facilitate start-ups was launched in Melbourne in 1979. This was followed by similar workshops being launched by universities, with school-based enterprise programs and university level courses in entrepreneurship and small business management delivered in different states from 1982 to 1990. Venture capital (VC) providers also emerged in the late 1980s with support from federal and state governments (Gillin, 1991).

The 1980s was therefore a launching pad for both SBP and EP within Australia and New Zealand. It was motivated by government recognition that economic change for both countries was necessary if employment and economic growth rates were to be sustained. The trends taking place in other countries were influential in shaping government policy in this period, particularly developments in the UK and USA. This helped to stimulate academic research and teaching in the small business and entrepreneurship domain, with the foundation of the Small Enterprise Association of Australia and New Zealand (SEAANZ) in 1987 providing a "Trans-Tasman" forum for the "four-pillars" of research, education, policy and practice to engage (Landström, 2005; Schaper, 2014). In Australia, the focus was on government intervention as illustrated by the creation of SBDCs, the New Enterprise Incentive Scheme (NIES) and the creation of small business ministerial portfolios at federal and state levels. However, in New Zealand the government sought a more hands-off, market-driven approach (Massey & Cameron, 1999). This era was also the start of a global transition from the *Schumpeter Mark II regime* "managed economy" model to the emergence of an "Entrepreneurial Economy" (OECD, 2010b). Attention was now being given to SBP/EP issues, in particular the delivery of business development services, financing and tentative initiatives designed to foster entrepreneurial culture.

Small business policy development in the 1990s

The momentum in the development of SBP and EP that commenced in the 1980s continued into the 1990s across both Australia and New Zealand. In Australia, the Hawke/Keating ALP government remained in office until 1996. The LNP coalition government of John Howard that replaced it remained in office until 2007 and placed a high emphasis on SBP and EP initiatives. In New Zealand, the 1990s was dominated by the NP governments of Prime Ministers Jim Bolger and his successor Jenny Shipley, which embraced free market forces and continued the process of economic reform.

During the final years of the Hawke/Keating ALP government there was a shift from SBP to EP-centric policy initiatives. Direct industry support was provided by the creation of Pooled Development Funds in 1992 and the program delivery arm AusIndustry in 1995. The Karpin Report of 1995 examined the international competitiveness of Australia's management and business leadership. While not solely focused on SBP/EP issues, it recommended the fostering of an "enterprising culture" through education programs at school and tertiary level in small business and entrepreneurship. The development of a "major community education program" targeted as promoting "the value of enterprise and entrepreneurial behaviour" was also recommended (Karpin, 1995a, 1995b). This report built on earlier work (e.g. Australian Manufacturing Council [AMC], 1994a, 1994b, 1995; Carmichael, 1994; LEK Partners, 1994) that emphasised the need for greater innovation, skills development and entrepreneurial growth within Australia's industries. These reports laid the foundation for future SBP/EP government initiatives as well as fostering academic research and education in the universities (Landström, 2005).

A key initiative of the Howard LNP government was the Small Business Deregulation Taskforce of 1996 and the publication of the Prime Minister's policy statement *More Time for Business* (Howard, 1997). This provided a blueprint for where the government wished to take the SME sector and with it the national economy. It focused on a range of SBP issues including taxation, removal of "red tape" compliance costs, industrial relations and unfair dismissal laws and access to finance. There were also some direct assistance measures including a Small Business Innovation Fund, R&D Start program, Technology Support Centres and enhanced support services from AusIndustry in R&D, commercialisation, business development and networking (Howard, 1997). At the same time a parliamentary inquiry into the imbalance between SMEs and large firms "Finding a Balance" reported on retail tenancy, franchising, abuses of market power and small business financing (Reid, 1997). These largely SBP focused reviews were complemented by a range of EP initiatives that included the establishment of the R&D Start Program and Innovation Investment Funds in 1997 targeted at high-growth SMEs (Schaper, 2014).

In New Zealand, the 1990s saw SBP coordinated by the Ministry of Commerce (later Ministry of Economic Development). A review of SBP programs undertaken in 1990 found that many existing schemes were not having the desired impact and that they were ineffective. This led to the restructuring of the Regional Development Commissions (RDCs) and BDBs with SBP becoming focused on regional development. The BDBs Act 1991 established these entities as independent crown agencies, considered to be better able to respond to the needs of SMEs. This led to the BDBs establishing Business Development Centres, akin to the BECs found in Australia and the UK, and managed grants and programs (Nyamori & Lawrence, 1997). However, the BDBs were eventually closed in 1998 (Jurado & Massey, 2012). This period also saw a focus within EP initiatives towards entrepreneurship amongst women, Maori and minority groups in the form of an Enterprise Assistance Program (Nyamori & Lawrence, 1997). These were primarily designed to reduce unemployment, but there was also the emergence of a strong EP focus with an emphasis on high-growth SMEs (Jurado & Massey, 2012).

The 1990s saw the continuation of the work commenced in the 1980s with further refinements and an increasing focus on EP-centric initiatives at the expense of SBP-centric ones. SBP initiatives continued to focus on the business enabling environment, business development services and financing issues as outlined in Figure 1. However, the desire for more employment and economic growth saw EP-centric initiatives emerge in relation to the fostering of an entrepreneurial culture, encouraging export market access and investment in technology and innovation. It was also a period in which there was a convergence of EP and innovation (science and technology) policy initiatives (Dodgson, Hughes, Foster, & Metcalfe, 2011). By the end of the century SMEs and entrepreneurship were researched and taught across most universities in Australia and New Zealand (Breen & Bergin, 1999; Crispin, McCauley, Dibben, Hoell, & Miles, 2013). Incubators and business support centres were operating widely (Kemp & Weber, 2012), and there was a dedicated small business journal *Small Enterprise Research: The Journal of SEAANZ* (established 1992) that provided an outlet for Australian and New Zealand academics. Indeed, Landström (2005) suggested that the journal has played an "important developmental role ... for entrepreneurship and small business research" in the two countries.

Small business policy development since 2000

The decade and a half since the start of the new millennium has seen SBP and EP follow a similar trajectory to that which emerged from the preceding two decades. With both nations' economies now restructured, deregulated and closely integrated, there was a continued expansion of EP-centric initiatives, particularly in New Zealand. The "Bright Future" innovation policy initially developed by the Shipley National government was adopted by the NZ Labour government of Prime Minister Helen Clark that came to power in 1999 (Jurado and Massey, 2012). This had a strong EP-centric focus with NZ $223 million in initiatives over four years including substantial investments in education with "enterprise education" courses delivered in schools and the "BIZ Programme" delivering management skills training. There was also a strong investment in scientific research, commercialisation and technology incubators. Additional measures including R&D tax incentives, "red tape" reduction, the creation of a "second board" on the NZ Stock Exchange for small firms, and inbound investment promotional strategies (Bradford, 1999). The creation of the international business development agency NZ Trade & Enterprise (NZTE) in 2003 also signalled a strong focus on high-growth entrepreneurship targeting "Gazelles" and "Born Global" SMEs.

In 2012 the MBIE was created by the National government of Prime Minister John Key. This agency brought together former Ministries and Departments responsible for employment, economic development, building and housing, tourism, education, plus science and innovation. Within this "super" Ministry, responsibility for SMEs was shared across portfolios held by 18 Ministers. While retaining a Minister of Small Business and revamping the SBAG, the focus on SMEs specifically was replaced by a commitment to creating an enabling environment for all businesses. Following a period of sector consultation, MBIE released a future-focussed National Statement of Science and Investment (NSSI) for the period 2015–2025 (MBIE, 2015). This articulates a vision for New Zealand to develop a strong national innovation system with EP-centric initiatives targeted at primary industries, ICT, manufacturing, environment and health. As MBIE also oversees the New Zealand business regulatory system, it has continued to provide SBP-centric programs including information and advisory services to SMEs. The www.business.govt.nz website has been developed as a significant resource for New Zealand businesses and contributes to New Zealand being ranked in second place in the World Bank's "ease of doing business" rankings (World Bank, 2016b). There are also private mentoring services available such as those run by the not-for-profit Business Mentors New Zealand (BMNZ), founded in 1991 (BMNZ, 2016). In addition, there are many other groups, programs and initiatives now encompassing SMEs and the support of entrepreneurs including a range of education programs at all levels of the school system and into the universities. Technology incubators and commercialisation support centres have also been developed with key links to the universities and publicly funded research centres as part of the government's focus on the creation of an enabling environment for entrepreneurial growth and development.

Australia's approach to SBP/EP initiatives in the first decade were shaped by the policy framework outlined by the "More Time for Business" statement (Howard, 1997). This included EP-centric initiatives such as the establishment of Commercialising Emerging Technologies (COMET) program launched in 2000, and the SBP-centric initiatives involving amendments to the *Trade Practices Act, 2006, Independent Contractor's Act, 2006,* and the Small Business Enterprise Program (SBEP) targeted at management and skills development in established SMEs. The election of the ALP government of Prime Minister Kevin Rudd in 2007 coincided with the GFC and this led to initiatives at both federal and state level to assist existing businesses. The "Enterprise Connect" program launched in 2008 was an initiative designed to provide support to established SMEs seeking to grow and involved benchmarking, consulting and co-funding for management positions.

The establishment of the DIISR in 2007 was designed to concentrate the necessary policy resources for SBP and EP, as well as science and innovation into the one agency. This was built on a steady development of innovation policy that commenced with the Howard LNP coalition government's *Backing Australia's Ability* report of 2001 (Department of Communications, Information, Technology and the Arts [DCITA], 2004), which outlined a national policy platform for enhancing Australia's international competitiveness through science and innovation. The Cutler Report of 2008 reviewed Australia's national innovation system (NIS) and made wide-ranging recommendations for improvement, particularly the relationship between universities and other publicly funded research centres and industry. The Rudd ALP government's 2009 policy statement *Powering Ideas* outlined further initiatives for building Australia's NIS (Carr, 2009). The difference between the policy statements of 2001 and 2009 was essentially a shift from a relatively narrow focus on government support for research and innovation, to a more holistic approach recognising the need to connect innovation and research with industry, business and government policy (Dodgson et al., 2011). Other initiatives within this period, which were continued by Rudd's successor Prime Minister Julia Gillard, were the placement of the federal Small Business Minister within the inner cabinet in 2012 and the appointment of the first national Small Business Commissioner in the same year (Mazzarol & Kemp, 2012). This appointment followed a trend across many states and territories where Small Business Commissioners had been appointed during the previous decade (Mazzarol, 2012).

The election of the LNP coalition government of Prime Minister Tony Abbott in 2013 brought a strong focus on SBP led by federal Small Business Minister Bruce Billson. The LNP coalition came into office on a platform of 23 policy initiatives focusing on enhanced advocacy for SMEs, regulatory reform to help cut "red tape", tax cuts for SMEs, direct assistance in relation to employment and tax laws, as well as infrastructure investments (Mazzarol, 2013). This agenda was pursued for the first two years and saw the establishment of an Australian Small Business and Family Enterprise Ombudsman (ASBFEO) under its own federal *ASBEFO Act, 2015*. The change of Prime Minister from Abbott to

Malcolm Turnbull in 2015 saw the departure of Billson from Cabinet and a shift in focus from SBP to EP-centric initiatives. This took the form of policy announcements promoting entrepreneurial start-ups and the launch of the National Innovation and Science Agenda in December of that year (Mazzarol, 2015).

By 2016 SBP and EP within Australia and New Zealand had transformed into holistic national strategies that were mainstream central policy platforms. They encompassed all the six fields outlined in the SME Policy Framework shown in Figure 1 and were becoming more integrated. The importance of entrepreneurship was recognised at the national level and had emerged as a major focus for universities and other education institutions. The economies of the two nations were now open and highly dependent on global trade and the free flow of capital, goods and people. In terms of global competitiveness both countries were well ranked with New Zealand ranked second in the world, behind Singapore, in terms of its 'ease of doing business' (World Bank, 2016b). Australia, by comparison ranked 13th out of 189 countries for the ease of doing business (World Bank, 2016a). The Global Innovation Index report of 2015 also placed New Zealand in 15th place and Australia in 17th place out of a total of 141 nations (Dutta, Lanvin, & Wunsch-Vincent, 2015).

Conclusions, implications and future outlook

This review of the evolution of SBP/EP in Australia and New Zealand over the past 46 years shows an increasing level of sophistication and maturing within the development of policy for SMEs. Despite some minor differences the pattern of evolution found within both nations has been similar, due in most part to their close economic and social ties, as well as their tendency to look at international trends and adopt them. The economic reforms of the 1980s and 1990s helped to address many of the regulatory and structural issues associated with the creation of a business enabling environment. As noted above, both nations now rank highly in global performance measures for ease of doing business and innovation. However, many issues remain, particularly relating to the need to provide more balance and equity for SMEs when dealing with large firms (Reid, 1997) and how SMEs navigate the complexities of regulations relating to employment, business establishment, closure and transfer and other compliances (see Lignier, Evans, & Tran-Nam, 2014; Lyons, Mortimer, Whiting, & Wilkinson, 2007; Productivity Commission, 2013, 2015a, 2015b, 2015c; Samujh, 2008). The provision of start-up counselling, business development services and small business training is an ongoing issue, with major concerns over whether such direct initiatives are best provided by the government or private sector, and even whether they are effective or even necessary (Dawe & Nguyen, 2007; Lee & McGuiggan, 2009; Mitchell, 2007; Webster, Walker, & Brown, 2005).

Access to credit and financing also remains an issue for SMEs. However, it is an area that divides between SBP and EP. For example, most SME owner-managers favour retained earnings over debt, and debt over shared equity as a means of financing (Watson & Wilson, 2002). Although this makes rapid growth difficult, it is a sensible and sustainable approach to the management of a business. SBP initiatives that can help SMEs to reduce costs or increase profitability (e.g. tax cuts, reduced compliance and input costs) will have the most positive impact on SME financing. However, for the minority of high-growth "Gazelle" firms, the need for equity funding, particularly

(VC, remains very important. Australia has a relatively small VC market (ABS, 2010) and there is a relative lack of such funding at the early "pre-seed" and "seed" stages (Jones, 2008). Attempts to create VC funds in Australia from the early 1990s had mixed outcomes, and despite the passage of time the availability of VC remains low (particularly for early-stage ventures). This has resulted in the "leakage" of entrepreneurs and innovators to other countries (Ferris AO, 2001).

Considerably more has been achieved over recent decades concerning the fostering of an entrepreneurial culture. Business incubators and start-up accelerators have or are being established in both countries. For example, in Australia there is a strong focus within almost all universities towards entrepreneurship with degree programs and research centres (Maritz, Jones, & Shwetzer, 2015). Entrepreneurship and innovation are also championed within government policy, and this is increasingly integrated into innovation and technology initiatives designed to enhance the level of commercialisation from public investment in research (Business Council of Australia [BCA], 2004, 2006). In many respects this pattern of SME policy evolution is akin to that taking place around the world (Osimo, 2016). It also parallels the experience of SME policy evolution in the UK (May & McHugh, 2002).

Implications for research and policy development

Although the general trajectory of SBP/EP in Australia and New Zealand is positive, many questions remain unanswered. Research into the effectiveness of policies designed to enhance the entrepreneurial culture and foster new venture creation, particularly through education, remains inconclusive (Henry, Hill, & Leitch, 2005a, 2005b; Rigby & Ramlogan, 2013). Analysis of labour market data suggests that a small proportion of "Gazelles" are major generators of net new jobs (Birch, 1987; Hendrickson et al., 2015; Wiens & Jackson, 2015). However, not all such firms are high-tech "Silicon Valley Business Model" ventures (Hendrickson et al., 2015). There is also a lack of reliable evidence to suggest that public policy initiatives promoting start-ups will result in more jobs (Davis, Haltiwanger, & Schuh, 1994; Nightingale & Coad, 2014; Shane, 2009). In fact, the available evidence suggests that most start-ups will not generate jobs and the jobs they do create will be of poor quality (Acs et al., 2016; Davila et al., 2015).

For researchers and policy-makers the challenge is to look past the allure of the atypical high-impact outliers such as "Gazelles", "Born Globals" and "Unicorns",[1] and focus on the behaviour of most SMEs. Although "ordinary" SMEs are less exciting, they remain the overwhelming bulk of all firms within an economy. Even though such firms are not growth focused, they can make a strong contribution to the national economy and employment base. For example, in Australia SMEs employ 70.5% of the workforce and the micro and small firms contribute nearly half of the nation's jobs. Out of a total workforce of 11.5 million, more than 8 million are employed by SMEs (Gilfillan, 2015). If even a half of these SMEs could be encouraged to grow and employ just one additional employee the total impact on employment would be significant. Germany's economic growth has been driven by its *Mittelstand* (Simon, 1992). Such firms are typically globally focused, but privately owned and locally embedded, with rates of growth that are steady and sustainable without the need for third-party equity (Audretsch & Elston, 1997).

Public policy designed to target this type of incremental growth in the SME sector has been referred to as "Economic Gardening" (EG), targeted as "second stage" established firms with between 10 and 99 employees (Braun, Harman, & Paton, 2014). Rather than promoting start-ups with their inherent risk, EG focuses on assisting established SMEs to grow through the provision of resources they might require to make strategic decisions about new product development and new market entry. EG emphasizes local initiatives designed to support the sustainability and growth of all firms in a region rather than targeting a select few (Barrios & Barrios, 2004). It follows an ecosystem approach in which regional industries are strengthened and made more resilient through clustering, networking, business needs assessments, market analysis and building on the existing strengths of the firms and industries already operating (Desplaces, Wergeles, & McGuigan, 2009). While not a solution to all economic policy challenges it offers a lower risk alternative to the current focus on hunting high-tech "Gazelles" and the even more elusive "Unicorns".

Concluding comments

Regardless of the approach, there is a need for much better evidence over the relative costs and benefits of SBP and EP initiatives. As has been shown in this historical review of the evolution of SME policy in Australia and New Zealand over the past four and half decades, many different policies and programs have been tried. Some have disappeared without a trace and others continue to operate. Many were found to have failed to deliver, but most were the victims of changed political dogma. Among the lessons that might be drawn from this historical analysis is that building effective SME policy takes time and is largely indirect in nature. There are few quick fixes and "magic bullet" solutions. As Storey (2008) notes, "macro" policies (e.g. immigration policy, competition policy, regulation, taxation and infrastructure) are more likely to have success than "micro" policies (e.g. training, support and advisory services). Evidence-based policy development supported by objective evaluation of any programs is essential and ideological, faddish prescriptions should be avoided. Investing in a national strategic research agenda on SMEs would enable the collection and evaluation of relevant data over time to underpin decisions on effective economic policies and programs.

Note

1. Unicorn refers to a business that is less than 10 years old but is valued at over 1 billion dollars.

References

Acs, Z., Astebro, T. B., Audretsch, D. B., & Robinson, D.T. (2016). *Public policy to promote entrepreneurship: A call to arms.* Retrieved from http://papers.ssrn.com/sol3/papers.cfm?abstract_id = 2728664 Duke I&E Research Paper No. 16-9; HEC Paris Research Paper No. SPE-2016–1137.
Anglund, S. M. (2000). *Small business policy and the American creed.* Westport, Conn.: Praeger.
Attard, B. (2008). The economic history of Australia from 1788: An introduction. In R. Whaples (Ed.), *EH.Net encyclopedia.* Retrieved from http://eh.net/encyclopedia/the-economic-history-of-australia-from-1788-an-introduction/

Audretsch, D. B., & Elston, J. A. (1997). Financing the German Mittelstand. *Small Business Economics*, *9*(2), 97–110.

Australian Bureau of Statistics. (2002). *Small business in Australia 2001*. Canberra: Australian Bureau of Statistics, Cat. 1321.0, Commonwealth of Australia.

Australian Bureau of Statistics. (2010). *Venture capital and later stage private equity, Australia*. Canberra: Australian Bureau of Statistics AGPS.

Australian Manufacturing Council. (1994a). *Leading the way: A study of best manufacturing practice in Australia and New Zealand*. Melbourne: Author.

Australian Manufacturing Council. (1994b). *The wealth of ideas: How linkages help sustain innovation and growth*. Melbourne: Author.

Australian Manufacturing Council. (1995). *The innovation cycle: Practical tips from innovative firms*. Melbourne: Author.

Barrios, S., & Barrios, D. (2004). Reconsidering economic development: The prospects for economic gardening. *Public Administration Quarterly*, *28*(1/2), 70–101.

Bean, J. J. (2000). Small business policy and the American creed. *Business History Review*, *74*(3), 538–540.

Beddall, D. P. (1990). *Small business in Australia: Challenges, problems and opportunities*. Canberra: Report by the House of Representatives Standing Committee on Industry, Science and Technology, Australian Government Publishing Service.

Bennett, R. J. (2014). *Entrepreneurship, small business and public policy: Evolution and revolution*. Florence: Taylor & Francis.

Berghoff, H. (2006). The end of family business? The Mittelstand and German capitalism in transition, 1949–2000. *The Business History Review*, *80*(2), 263–295.

Birch, D. (1979). *The job generation process*. Retrieved from SSRN: http://ssrn.com/abstract = 1510007, MIT Program on Neighbourhood and Regional Change Vol, 302.

Birch, D. (1987). *Job creation in America: How our small companies put the most people to work*. New York, NY: The Free Press.

Blackbourn, D. (1977). The Mittelstand in German society and politics, 1871–1914. *Social History*, *2*(4), 409–433.

Blackburn, R. A., & Schaper, M. T. (2012). *Government SMEs and entrepreneurship development: Policy, practice and challenges*. Farnham, UK: Gower.

Blackford, M. G. (2003). *A history of small business in America second edition*. Chapel Hill: University of North Carolina Press.

Bolton, J. E. (1971). *Small firms: Report of the committee of inquiry on small firms*. London: HM Stationery Office.

Bolton, J. E. (1982). The future of small businesses: A review of developments since the committee of inquiry (1969–71). *Journal of the Royal Society of Arts*, *130*(5310), 305–320.

Bordo, M., Hargreaves, D., & Kida, M. (2011). Global shocks, economic growth and financial crises: 120 years of New Zealand experience. *Financial History Review*, *18*(3), 331–355.

Bradford, M. (1999). *Speech to the economic development associations of New Zealand conference*. Retrieved from beehive.govt.nz https://www.beehive.govt.nz/speech/speech-economic-development-associations-new-zealand-conference, Government of New Zealand

Braun, P., Harman, J., & Paton, F. (2014). Economic gardening: Capacity building for stronger regions. *Journal of Economic and Social Policy*, *16*(1), 1–27.

Breen, J., & Bergin, S. (1999). *Small business and entrepreneurship education in Australian universities*. . Melbourne: Small Business Research Unit, Victoria University of Technology.

Bridge, S. (2010). *Rethinking enterprise policy: Can failure trigger new understanding?* Houndmills, Basingstoke, Hampshire: Palgrave Macmillan.

Business Council of Australia. (2004). *Building effective systems for the commercialisation of university research*. Melbourne: Allen Consulting Group, Business Council of Australia and the Australian Vice Chancellors' Committee.

Business Council of Australia. (2006). *New concepts in innovation: The keys to a growing Australia*. Melbourne: Author.

Business Mentors New Zealand. (2016). *Business Mentors New Zealand Limited*. Retrieved from http://www.businessmentors.org.nz/.

Carmichael, L. (1994). *The shape of things to come: Small business employment and skills*. Canberra: Australian Government Publishing Service.

Carr, K. (2009). *Powering ideas: An innovation agenda for the 21st century*. Canberra: Commonwealth of Australia.

Crispin, S., McCauley, A., Dibben, M., Hoell, R., & Miles, M. (2013). To teach or try: A continuum of approaches to entrepreneurship education in Australasia. *American Journal of Entrepreneurship, 6*(2), 94–109.

Dahlstrand, A. L., & Stevenson, L. (2007). *Linking innovation and entrepreneurship policy*. Stockholm: Swedish Foundation for Small Business, Innovative Policy Research for Economic Growth (IPREG).

Davila, A., Foster, G., He, X., & Shimizu, C. (2015). The rise and fall of startups: Creation and destruction of revenue and jobs by young companies. *Australian Journal of Management, 40*(1), 6–35.

Davis, S. J., Haltiwanger, J., & Schuh, S. (1994). Small business and job creation: Dissecting the myth and reassessing the facts. *Business Economics, 29*(3), 13–21.

Dawe, S., & Nguyen, N. (2007). *Education and training that meets the needs of small business: A systematic review of research*. Adelaide: National Centre for Vocational Education Research.

Department of Communications, Information, Technology and the Arts. (2004). *Backing Australia's ability: Building our future through science and innovation*. Canberra: Department of Communications, Information, Technology and the Arts, Commonwealth of Australia.

Department of Foreign Affairs and Trade (2016). *Australia-New Zealand closer economic relations trade agreement*. Department of Foreign Affairs and Trade. www.dfat.gov.au Australian Government.

Department of Innovation, Industry, Science and Research. (2011). *Key statistics: Australian small business*. AGPS Canberra: Department of Innovation, Industry, Science and Research.

Desplaces, D. E., Wergeles, F., & McGuigan, P. (2009). Economic gardening through entrepreneurship education: A service-learning approach. *Industry and Higher Education, 23*(6), 473–484.

Devlin, M., & Le Heron, R. B. (1977). *Report to the development finance corporation on dimensions of New Zealand business*. Palmerston North: Massey University Research Group.

Dodgson, M., Hughes, A., Foster, J., & Metcalfe, S. (2011). Systems thinking, market failure, and the development of innovation policy: The case of Australia. *Research Policy, 40*(9), 1145–1156.

Dutta, S., Lanvin, B., & Wunsch-Vincent, S. (2015). *The global innovation index 2015: Effective innovation policies for development*. Fontainebleau, Ithaca and Geneva: Cornell University, INSEAD, WIPO.

Ferris AO, W. D. (2001). Australia chooses: Venture capital and a future Australia. *Australian Journal of Management, 26*(Special Issue), 45–64.

Gilfillan, G. (2015). Statistical snapshot: Small business employment contribution and workplace arrangements. *Parliamentary Library Research Paper Series, 2015–16*, Parliament of Australia.

Gillin, L. M. (1991). Entrepreneurship education: The Australian perspective for the nineties. *Journal of Small Business & Entrepreneurship, 9*(1), 60–72.

Hendrickson, L., Bucifal, S., Balaguer, A., & Hansell, D. (2015). *The employment dynamics of Australian entrepreneurship; research paper 4/2015*. Retrieved from www.industry.gov.au/Office-of-the-Chief-Economist/Research-Papers/Documents/, Office of the Chief Scientist, Department of Industry and Science, Australian Government.

Henry, C., Hill, F., & Leitch, C. (2005a). Entrepreneurship education and training: Can entrepreneurship be taught? Part I. *Education + Training, 47*(2), 98–111.

Henry, C., Hill, F., & Leitch, C. (2005b). Entrepreneurship education and training: Can entrepreneurship be taught? Part II. *Education & Training, 47*(3), 158–169.

Howard, J. W. (1997). *More time for business*. Canberra: Australian Government Publishing Service.

Jones, A. (2008). Venture capital in Australia. *Chemistry in Australia, 75*(6), 12–14.

Jurado, T., & Massey, C. (2012). SME policy development in New Zealand 1978–2008. In R. A. Blackburn, & M. T. Schaper (Eds.), *Government SMEs and entrepreneurship development: Policy, practice and challenges* (pp. 33–46). Farnham, UK, Gower (Chapter 3).

Karpin, D. (1995a). *Enterprising nation: Renewing Australia's managers to meet the challenges of the Asia-pacific century – report to the industry task force on leadership and management skills, volume 1.* Canberra: Commonwealth of Australia.

Karpin, D. (1995b). *Enterprising nation: Renewing Australia's managers to meet the challenges of the Asia-pacific century - report to the industry task force on leadership and management skills, volume 2.* Canberra: Commonwealth of Australia.

Kemp, P., & Weber, P. (2012). Business incubators: Their genesis, forms, intent and impact. In R. A. Blackburn, & M. T. Schaper (Eds.), *Government SMEs and entrepreneurship development: Policy, practice and challenges* (pp. 149–164). Farnham: Gower (Chapter 8).

Landström, H. (2005). *Pioneers in entrepreneurship and small business research.* Boston: Springer.

Lee, G., & McGuiggan, R. (2009). Small business training needs, preferred channels, and barriers. *Journal of Academy of Business and Economics, 9*(2), 103–115.

LEK Partnership. (1994). *Intelligent exports and the silent revolution in services: A report.* Sydney: Australian Trade Commission.

Lignier, P., Evans, C., & Tran-Nam, B. (2014). Tangled up in tape: The continuing tax compliance plight of the small and medium enterprise business sector. *Australian Tax Forum, 29*(2), 217–247.

Lundström, A., & Stevenson, L. A. (2010). *Entrepreneurship policy: Theory and practice.* New York, NY: Springer.

Lundström, A., Vikström, P., Fink, M., Meuleman, M., Głodek, P., Storey, D., & Kroksgård, A. (2014). Measuring the costs and coverage of SME and entrepreneurship policy: A pioneering study. *Entrepreneurship Theory and Practice, 38*(4), 941–957.

Lyons, M., Mortimer, D., Whiting, E., & Wilkinson, F. (2007). Small and medium establishments and the new federal workplace relations system. *Employment Relations Record, 7*(1), 37–50.

Maritz, A., Jones, C., & Shwetzer, C. (2015). The status of entrepreneurship education in Australian universities. *Education+Training, 57*(8/9), 1020–1035.

Mason, C., & Brown, R. (2014). *Entrepreneurial ecosystems and growth oriented entrepreneurship. The Hague.* Netherlands: OECD LEED Programme and the Dutch Ministry of Economic Affairs.

Massey, C., & Cameron, A. (1999). Government assistance to New Zealand SMEs: Ideological purity of political pragmatism. *Small Enterprise Research, 7*(2), 43–54.

Massey, C., & Ingley, C. (2007). *The New Zealand environment for the development of SMEs. The New Zealand centre for SME research report,* ISBN 978-0-9582810-1-0, NZ SME Centre, Massey University, Wellington, New Zealand, p. 27.

May, T., & McHugh, J. (2002). Small business Policy: A Political Consensus? *The Political Quarterly, 73*(1), 76–85.

Mazzarol, T. (2012). Small business finally has a national profile, but will it have the power? *The Conversation.* Retrieved from https://theconversation.com/small-business-finally-has-a-national-profile-but-will-it-have-the-power-5845, www.theconversation.com

Mazzarol, T. (2013). Small business policy – where do the two main parties stand? *The Conversation.* Retrieved from https://theconversation.com/small-business-policy-where-do-the-two-main-parties-stand-17294, www.theconversation.com

Mazzarol, T. (2015). Will the national innovation and science agenda deliver Australia a world class national innovation system? *The Conversation.* Retrieved from https://theconversation.com/will-the-national-innovation-and-science-agenda-deliver-australia-a-world-class-national-innovation-system-52081, www.theconversation.com.

Mazzarol, T., & Kemp, P. (2012). An open letter to Brendan O'Connor – how to 'get' small business. *The Conversation.* Retrieved from https://theconversation.com/an-open-letter-to-brendan-oconnor-how-to-get-small-business-5692, www.theconversaation.com.

Ministry of Business, Innovation and Employment. (2015). *National statement of science and investment 2012-2025.* Wellington www.mbie.govt.nz, Ministry of Business, Innovation and Employment, New Zealand Government.

Ministry of Business, Innovation and Employment. (2016). *Small businesses in New Zealand: How do they compare with larger firms?* Wellington: Ministry of Business, Innovation & Employment, Government of New Zealand.

Meredith, G. G. (1993). *Small business management in Australia* (4th ed.). Sydney: McGraw-Hill.

Mitchell, J. (2007). *Overcoming "I'm too busy": An audit of small business training in Western Australia*. Perth: Department of Education and Training, Government of Western Australia.

Nightingale, P., & Coad, A. (2014). Muppets and gazelles: Political and methodological biases in entrepreneurship research. *Industrial and Corporate Change, 23*(1), 113–143.

Nyamori, R., & Lawrence, S. (1997). Small business policy in New Zealand. *New Zealand Journal of Business, 19*(1&2), 73–93.

Organisation for Economic Co-operation and Development. (2004). *SME statistics: Towards a more systematic statistical measurement of SME behaviour. Promoting entrepreneurship and innovative SMEs in a global economy.* Istanbul Turkey: Author, Paris.

Organisation for Economic Co-operation and Development. (2006). *Governance of innovation systems volume 3: Case studies in cross-sectoral policy.* Paris: Author.

Organisation for Economic Co-operation and Development. (2010a). *High-growth enterprises: What governments can do to make a difference.* Paris: Author.

Organisation for Economic Co-operation and Development. (2010b). *SMEs, entrepreneurship and innovation.* Paris: Author.

Osimo, D. (2016). *The 2016 start-up nation scoreboard: How European union countries are improving policy frameworks and developing powerful ecosystems for entrepreneurs.* Lisbon: The Lisbon Council and Neats.

Productivity Commission. (2013). *Regulator engagement with small business.* Melbourne: Author, Government of Australia.

Productivity Commission. (2015a). *Business set-up, transfer and closure: Productivity commission inquiry report no. 75, 30 September 2015.* Canberra: AGPS.

Productivity Commission. (2015b). *Workplace relations framework: Productivity commission inquiry report volume 1 No. 76.* Canberra: Australian Government, Productivity Commission.

Productivity Commission. (2015c). *Workplace relations framework: Productivity commission inquiry report volume 2 No. 76.* Canberra: Australian Government, Productivity Commission.

Reid, B. (1997). *Finding a balance: Towards fair trading in Australia.* Canberra: Parliament of the Commonwealth of Australia.

Rigby, J., & Ramlogan, R. (2013). *The impact and effectiveness of entrepreneurship policy* (NESTA working paper, *13*(1)). Retrieved from www.nesta.org.uk/wp13-01.

Samujh, H. (2008). Government consults small business on business compliance costs: A New Zealand experience. *Small Enterprise Research: The Journal of SEAANZ, 16*(2), 45–59.

Schaper, M. (2014). A brief history of small business in Australia, 1970–2010. *Journal of Entrepreneurship and Public Policy, 3*(2), 222–236.

Shane, S. (2009). Why encouraging more people to become entrepreneurs is bad public policy. *Small Business Economics, 33*(2), 141–149.

Simon, H. (1992). Lessons from Germany's midsize giants. *Harvard Business Review, 70*(2), 115–123.

Singleton, J. (2008). New Zealand in the nineteenth and twentieth centuries. In R. Whaples (Ed.), *EH.Net encyclopedia.* Retrieved from http://eh.net/encyclopedia/an-economic-history-of-new-zealand-in-the-nineteenth-and-twentieth-centuries/

Sirolli, E. (2004). *Local enterprise facilitation* (Doctoral thesis). Murdoch University.

Storey, D. (2008). *Entrepreneurship and SME policy* (2008 Edition). Evian: World Entrepreneurship Forum.

Thurik, R. (2009). Entreprenomics: Entrepreneurship, economic growth, and policy. In Z. Acs, D. Audretsch, & R. Strom (Eds.), *Entrepreneurship, growth, and public policy* (pp. 219–249). Cambridge: Cambridge University Press.

Tuerck, D. G., Ahiakpor, J. C. W., Fitzroy, F. R., Latona J. C., & Foray D. (1990). Job creation in America: How our smallest companies put the most people to work. *Small Business Economics, 2*(1), 77–86.

United Nations Conference on Trade and Development. (2012). *Entrepreneurship policy framework and implementation guidance.* New York: Author.

Von Saldern, A. (1992). The old Mittelstand 1890–1939: How "backward" were the artisans? *Central European History, 25*(1), 27–51.

Watson, R., & Wilson, N. (2002). Small and medium sized enterprise financing: A note on some of the empirical implications of a pecking order. *Journal of Business Finance & Accounting, 29*(3/4), 557–578.

Webster, B., Walker, E., & Brown, A. (2005). Australian small business participation in training activities. *Education & Training, 47*(8/9), 552–561.

Wiens, J., & Jackson, C. (2015). *The importance of young firms for economic growth.* Kansas: Kauffman Foundation.

Wiltshire, F. M. (1974). *Report of the committee on small business, June 1971.* Canberra Australia: Parliamentary paper, no. 82 of 1973; Department of Trade and Industry.

World Bank. (2016a). *Doing business 2016: Measuring regulatory quality and efficiency – economy profile Australia.* Washington, DC: International Bank for Reconstruction and Development/The World Bank.

World Bank. (2016b). *Doing business 2016: Measuring regulatory quality and efficiency – economy profile New Zealand.* Washington, DC: International Bank for Reconstruction and Development/ The World Bank.

Ye, L., Tweed, D., & Toulson, P. (2012). SME policies and seasons of change in the People's Republic of China. In R. A. Blackburn, & M.T. Schaper (Eds.), *Government SMEs and entrepreneurship development: Policy, practice and challenges* (pp. 113–130). Farnham: Gower (Chapter 8).

Small and medium-sized enterprises policy in Korea from the 1960s to the 2000s and beyond

Chang-Yong Sung, Ki-Chan Kim and Sungyong In

ABSTRACT

Korea's economic growth is a truly remarkable one from its very humble beginning. The development and growth of small and medium-sized enterprises (SMEs) and their government policy are briefly examined herein. In short, in the 1960s and 1970s, the government policy was to help the development of SMEs, but focused on the heavy and chemical industries. In the 1980s and 1990s, many SMEs became key suppliers of various parts in the growing automobile and electronics industries. In the 2000s, various policies and initiatives for SMEs led to an explosive increase and growth of venture businesses. In the 2010s, a 'win–win' growth philosophy between large companies and SMEs was actively sought through promotions of various policies. Also, numerous efforts were made to strengthen the innovative competency of SMEs, establish fair-trading order, protect SME business area, actively promote win–win growth strategy and support for strengthening SMEs' autonomy.

Introduction

Over a relatively short time (i.e. four decades), Korea has achieved enormous success in building and transforming its economy into one of the global economic powers. This is often touted as the 'Korean miracle' in the modern history. Such a remarkable development has resulted in many success stories across all sectors of Korea, including politics, society and culture.

In the early 1950s, Korea had a mere subsistence economy which was close to nothing right after the Korean War from 1950 to 1953. The Korean War devastated the country and its economy, leaving the country as one of the poorest nations in the world at that time. Over the next five decades, however, Korea rose from the ashes of the Korean War and became a home for over 3 million large and small companies that compete globally, transforming its economy into a technology-based industrial economy. In this short paper, it is attempted to examine how such economic growth of Korea was made possible through various concerted efforts by both government and private sectors alike, from a perspective of the implementations of government policies for Small and medium-sized enterprises (SMEs). Further, in the following sections, this paper examines how SMEs were nurtured and developed, as well as their contributions to the growth of the Korean national economy from the 1950s to the 2000s, from a viewpoint of SME policy implementation by the government. The paper will also examine how the policy for SMEs in Korea brought about the changes, for fostering and growing them, as well as the outcomes and problems that Korean SMEs now face.

In short, in the 1960s and 1970s, the government policy for SMEs was to help the development of SMEs, through various five-year economic development plans, which were focused on the nurturing of the heavy and chemical industries. In the 1980s and 1990s, many SMEs became key suppliers of various parts and/or components in the growing automobile and electronics industries, elevating the status of SMEs from those in the labor-intensive light industry. In the 2000s, various policies and initiatives for SMEs led to an explosive increase and growth of venture businesses which later played a pivotal role in the revitalization of the Korean national economy. Further, in the 2010s, a 'win–win' growth philosophy or mandate between large companies and SMEs was actively sought through promotions of various business-friendly policies. Also, in the face of many daunting challenges on a global scale, numerous efforts have been made to strengthen the innovative competencies of SMEs which many policy-makers believed are in line with the future roles of SMEs in Korea (Choi, 2007).

Overview of Korea's economic development with SME policies

Figure 1 illustrates an overview of Korea's economic development from the 1960s to the 2000s with the main government policies for SMEs highlighted. As shown in Figure 1, the

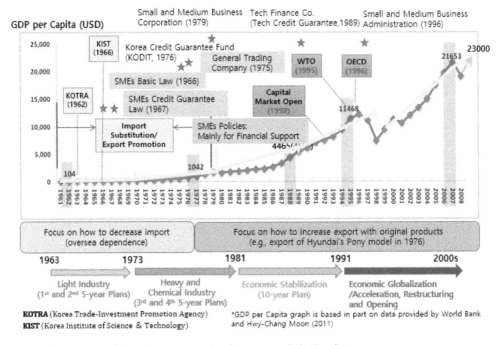

Figure 1. Overview of Korea's economic development with SME policies.

period of Korea's economic development may be broken into four periods of time from the 1960s to the 2000s: a first period for developing the light industry (from 1963 to 1973), a second period for developing the heavy and chemical industry (from 1973 to 1981), a third period for stabilizing the national economy (from 1981 to 1991) and a fourth period for globalizing the national economy (from 1991 to the 2000s). Each of these four periods may be characterized by different policy emphasis for large and small companies. For example, in the early 1960s to the late 1970s, the Korean government implemented what is called the 'five-year economic development plan' (e.g. the first, second, third and fourth five-year plans) to achieve different policy objectives. As the multiple five-year economic development plans were implemented by a step-by-step approach in the 1960s and 1970s, SMEs emerged and developed, which later grew to become the backbone of the Korean national economy in the later periods.

During the first and second five-year plans in the 1960s, the Korean government established the Korea Trade-Investment Promotion Agency (KOTRA) in 1962 to facilitate global trades and the Korea Institute of Science and Technology (KIST) to facilitate research and development of technology. Also, in 1966, SMEs Basic Law was enacted and promulgated as a first legal framework for SMEs in Korea and in 1967 the SME Credit Guarantee Law was enacted and promulgated as a foundation for providing financial support for SMEs. Further, in 1975, the government announced regulations relating to General Trading Company to provide SMEs with better access to the global market. The government also established the Korea Credit Guarantee Fund (KODIT) in 1976 and the Korea Small and Medium Business Corporation (SBC) in 1979. SBC is a non-profit, government-funded organization which implements government policies and programs for the development and growth of SMEs in Korea. KODIT is a public financial institution that provides comprehensive financial support for SMEs through general credit guarantees and business loans. During these early years of the 1960s and 1970s, SMEs mostly developed as subcontractors to large companies, and the government policies were designed and implemented to lessen overseas dependency by decreasing an amount of imports into the domestic market. Also, the emphasis and focus of the government policies were mostly on the development of the light industry in the 1960s and the heavy and chemical industry in the 1970s.

As the Korean national economy grew and the business and economic environment changed, the government policy also changed in the following decades. In the 1980s and 1990s, for example, the domestic environment and the international economic environment changed widely and rapidly to an extent that cannot be compared with other changes in the past. During these periods, the focus of the government policy shifted to stabilizing the national economy in the 1980s and globalization, restructuring, opening of markets and competition in the 1990s. In 1989, the government established Korea Technology Credit Guarantee Fund (KOTEC) to help and encourage technology-based projects by SMEs. KOTEC provides credit guarantees to help new technology-based enterprises or companies while promoting the growth of technology-based SMEs and venture businesses. Also, many policy implementations were made to increase exports with domestically developed, original products (e.g. Hyundai motor's Pony model vehicles).

In the 1990s, Korea experienced many changes. The capital market was opened for the first time in 1992. Korea joined the World Trade Organization (WTO) in 1995 and became a member country of the Organization for Economic Cooperation and Development in 1996. Also, in 1996, the Small and Medium Business Administration (SMBA) was established to help and support SMEs, and to be in line with the launch of the WTO, and the focus of the policy was shifted into a direction placing more emphasis on autonomy and open competition in the marketplace. Therefore, technology and knowledge became critical factors and played key roles in many industries, and management paradigm changes occurred, such as placing a high emphasis on corporate creativity and flexibility. While economic globalization was intensely promoted, SMEs generally continued to grow. However, in 1997, Korea experienced a very turbulent time due to the Asian financial crisis, resulting in a rapid decline in the number of SMEs. In fact, during the Asian financial crisis, numerous SMEs in Korea went technically bankrupt as many of their trading partners and large companies became insolvent (Heo, 2007).

By the early 2000s, the national economy began to rebound and overcame the Asian financial crisis by recovering from the set-back, achieving a remarkable growth reaching over 10% growth in 2010, which was accompanied by the promotion of the industrial development and growth of small and medium-sized ventures or companies. As evidenced from Figure 1 above, over a relatively short time, compared to other national economies, the Korean national economy became a global economy with an amazing track record of resilience and recovery from many challenging set-backs, which would not have been possible without the strengths of SMEs. What is also notable from Figure 1 is that, from a viewpoint of SME policy, from the 1960s to the 2000s, there has been an apparent shift in the focus of SME policy, which may be characterized as shown in Figure 2 below.

As shown in Figure 2, the government policy for SMEs appears to have gone through different phases over time, adapting to constantly changing environments in the marketplace. However, it has offered continuous investment in human capital which has been the foundation for many successful implementations of the SMEs policy, as well as for the growth of the Korean national economy in such a short time. The noted changes in the policy focus for SMEs may be characterized as follows. Initially, generating money or capital and laying the foundation for financial institutions and systems for SMEs was

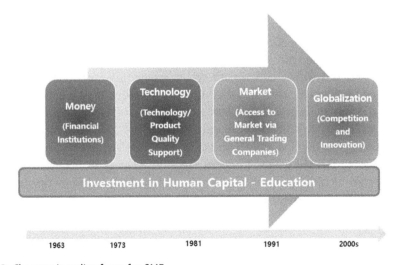

Figure 2. Changes in policy focus for SME.

the principal focus of the policy for SMEs. After the foundation for the financial institutions and systems for SMEs were in place, the focus of the policy for SMEs shifted to
the development of technology and support systems for building quality products for
the marketplace. Then, the policy focus for SMEs shifted to providing SMEs with access
to various markets which include both the domestic and overseas markets, and to the globalization of SMEs with focus on open competition and innovation.

Having briefly examined how the Korean economy developed over the past decades, a
more detailed examination of how SMEs contributed to the growth of the Korean national
economy and some of the performance results of related government policies are presented in the following sections (Lee, 2014a, 2014b).

Growth of Korean economy and roles of SMEs

One of the most important contributions of SMEs in Korea is that they have played a key
role in developing and maintaining the national economy in a healthy condition. Quan-
titatively, the SMEs ratio in the Korean national economy is huge. Based on 2005 statistics,
the ratios of SMEs and their employees (in percentage) are 99.8% and 88.1%, respectively.
During the growth process of the Korean national economy, SMEs' economic contribution
has been rising at a steady pace over the years as shown in Table 1 below. As can be seen in
Table 1, the economic development contribution rates for SMEs in terms of the number of
companies, the number of employees, output, shipment amount, and added value had
steadily increased over the years from 1960s to 2000s.

By way of example, the contribution of SMEs to employee numbers has increased
almost twofold from the 1980s (81.9%) compared to the 1970s (47.1%). The SME contributions to output, shipment amount and added value also approached 50% from the
1980s, exceeded 50% after the 1990s, and rose continuously thereafter. As can be seen
above, the contribution of SMEs to the Korean national economic development has steadily increased over time and has been playing a key role in building the national economy
and overcoming many economic crises that Korea faced in the past. For example, in the
late 1990s, when the Asian financial crisis occurred, the contribution rates of SMEs
exceeded those of large companies including conglomerates in terms of output, shipment
amount and added value. The contributions of SMEs to the development and growth of
the Korean national economy cannot be appreciated properly without a proper understanding of various government policies in place and implementations thereof in the

Table 1. Trends in rates of contribution of SMEs to Korean economic development (unit: %).

		1960s	1970s	1980s	1990s	2000s
No. of companies	SMEs	94.0	94.8	99.4	102.2	100.1
	Large	6.0	5.2	0.6	Δ2.2	Δ0.1
No. of employees	SMEs	38.1	47.1	81.9	Δ6.8	101.8
	Large	61.9	52.9	18.1	Δ93.2	Δ1.8
Output	SMEs	26.5	32.2	45.7	50.3	52.8
	Large companies	73.5	67.8	54.3	49.7	47.2
Shipment amount	SMEs	26.7	32.3	45.6	50.1	56.5
	Large	73.3	67.7	54.4	49.9	43.5
Added value	SMEs	25.7	35.7	47.7	50.5	56.0
	Large	74.3	64.3	52.3	49.5	44.0

Source: Korea National Statistical Office (2005).

past years. In the following sections, brief descriptions of various government policies and their implementations over past decades, from the 1960s to the 2010s, are provided to give a perspective on how SMEs in Korea faired under different policy implementations (Lee, 2006).

SMEs in the 1960s: industrialization policy implementation

In the 1960s, as noted above, the Korean government implemented its Industrialization Policy through multiple five-year economic development plans to build the national economy. During this period, industrialization progressed with a launch of focused economic development schemes. Economies of scale were regarded as important, and thus there was an increased emphasis on increasing the number of large scale factories. As such, the gap between large companies and SMEs widened. For example, many large companies grew rapidly with the implementation of government-led industrialization policy, but most SMEs did not benefit from the industrialization policy (SMEs relatively shrunk in size) (Seo, 2014). However, an Industrial Bank of Korea 1968 survey on the change in corporate size found that 61.8% of the surveyed large companies grew from SMEs in 1963 to large companies in 1968 (The Presidential Commission on Small and Medium Enterprises, 2007). As such, one may consider the growth of many SMEs into large companies as the development of the SME sector, which may be viewed as a reason for SMEs' relative shrinkage simultaneously. During this early period, as the industrialization progressed, the policies for SMEs started to have focus on a push into overseas markets and beyond the domestic markets. For example, the main emphasis of the policy was on the export of products from labor-intensive industries including textile, garment and leather goods, and other light manufacturing industries. Thus, by way of example, by 1971, the export of SMEs' products had risen sharply from 18.6% in 1963 to 32.4% in 1971. The enormous increase in the amount of exports by SMEs may be characterized as the most remarkable achievement in the development of SMEs in the 1960s.

SMEs in the 1970s: high growth through export policy

In the 1970s, the Korean national economy experienced an explosive growth period with export-focused government policies which implemented the nationalization of basic materials and the enhancement of structures for the export of goods. As such, government policy was focused on large companies and intensively fostered the development of the heavy and chemical industries. Because of a heavy emphasis on the development of large companies in the heavy and chemical industries, SMEs in this period were viewed as being relatively alienated and their economic status was weakened.

By the mid-1970s, the number of SMEs decreased and even technically bankrupt SMEs emerged during this period. In the latter part of the 1970s, however, the situation of SMEs began to improve. Towards the end of 1970s, the ratio of heavy and chemical industries rapidly increased relative to the small and medium-size manufacturing industry's structure. For example, many SMEs produced materials and/or parts or components for large companies in the heavy and chemical industries. Therefore, the production by SMEs of the materials or parts used for the heavy and chemical industries played a new role in supporting the production by large companies. Additionally, SMEs continuously maintained a high investment rate for production capacity-based expansion and facility modernization. As such, the 1970s can be characterized by notable improvements in the productivity of SMEs, often surpassing that of large companies, due to increased facility investment for labor reduction, facility improvement and the expansion of existing facilities. Although SMEs' added value productivity in 1974 was only 43.2% of that of large companies, by 1977 it rose to 82.1% of that of large companies.

SMEs in the 1980s: restructuring policy

In the 1980s, SMEs saw a turning point in their development process in Korea. During this time, Korea in general experienced a negative growth due to economic and social environmental changes, such as an oil shock and a financial crisis. In view of these changes, the Korean government implemented extensive restructuring policies in general, but put enormous efforts into cultivating and strengthening SMEs in the marketplace. By way of example, in terms of the number of employees and added value, the ratio of SMEs in the manufacturing industry rose from 49.6% and 35.2% in 1980 to 56.1% and 37.6%, respectively, in 1985. After 1986, the international balance of Korean economy turned into surplus, thanks to three factors – weak dollar, low oil price and low interest rate. With the help of these three factors, the Korean economy began to see high growth again and many SMEs become global or international companies. During this period of restructuring policy, SMEs began to emerge as the mainstream of the Korean national economy based on an advent of new industrial areas for SMEs, expansion of existing industrial areas through specialization, as well as corporate restructuring.

SMEs in the 1990s: economic shift policy

In the 1990s, SMEs emerged as key suppliers of automotive and electronics parts to large companies in the automotive and consumer electronics industries, moving the SME sector beyond the labor-intensive light industry, such as textile, garment and miscellaneous goods. Also, SMEs began to invest in information and technology development for their growth. By way of example, as the SMEs invested in the information and technology development, the ratio of technology development investment to sales rose from 0.19% to 0.34% in 1996. The average investment amount per SME sharply increased from KRW 20.1 million in 1989 to KRW 70.7 million in 1996. Further, as shown in Table 2 below, the export of SMEs increased. For example, from 1963 to 2006, the SME export ratio grew from 18.6% to 32% in general, posting about USD 104.1 billion.

In the 1990s, the number of SMEs continued to increase, while economic globalization progressed. By way of example, the number of SMEs in the manufacturing sector was

Table 2. Trends in Korean SMEs' export ratio (in percentage).

	1963	1965	1970	1975	1980	1983	1987	1990
SMEs export ratio	18.6	23.0	32.3	34.5	32.1	20.2	37.7	42.1
	1992	1994	1996	1998	2000	2002	2004	2006
SMEs export ratio	40.0	42.4	41.8	21.0	36.0	42.0	35.6	32.0

Source: KBIZ (Korea Federation of Small and Medium Business).

96,241, making up 99.1% of the total number of companies in Korea. At the same time, the number of employees at SMEs was about 2 million, which was about 69.2% of the total number of people employed in the country, and output from SMEs was 46.5%. These numbers were sharp increases compared to the figures in 1988, for example, 97.8% for the number of SMEs, 57.8% for the SME output and 39.4% for the number of people employed at SMEs. Also, as shown in Table 2 above, the SME export ratio dropped during the years of financial crisis. During this period of financial crisis, SMEs experienced a very difficult time because of the foreign exchange crisis, especially in 1997. For example, the number of SMEs (e.g. small and medium-sized manufacturers) in Korea fell 13.6% in a year from 78,869 in 1997 to 77,844 in 1998. Also, SMEs in Korea went through a stringent restructuring process, including financial structure improvement and productivity enhancement, and finally established themselves as the backbone of the country's economy by overcoming the financial crisis. Further, during this period, the Korean national economy saw numerous start-up activities (including many start-up companies) focused on commercialization of high-technology in various sectors. For example, the number of start-up employees surpassed 100,000 in 7 largest cities in Korea and the output reached KRW 12 trillion, with a sharp increase in the number of small and medium-sized start-ups, thereby building the foundation for the country's economic activity which significantly contributed to overcoming the financial crisis (KBIZ, 2007).

SMEs in the 2000s: fostering venture business

In the 2000s, the policy for SMEs may be characterized as being focused on the promotion of innovative SMEs (including new venture businesses). During this period, there was an explosive increase in the number of venture businesses, which contributed enormously to the revitalization of the Korean national economy. By way of example, in early 2000, the number of start-up businesses was 6547, which surpassed those of neighboring countries such as Japan and Taiwan. Further, start-up businesses in the information and computer-related areas constituted about 28.0% of the total number of start-up businesses. To this extent, new business opportunities were created for numerous SMEs in the new technology areas such as information, communication and the Internet (innovative SMEs). Innovative SMEs aimed to ensure global competitiveness based on a company's competence and enhanced qualitative competitiveness of their products and/or services, providing a new role model for SMEs in the Korean economy. By way of example, in 2006, the number of innovative SMEs was 17,000, which increased by more than twofold, compared to that in 2003. Also, innovative SMEs posted a 2.6 times higher ratio in terms of job creation and a 3.2 times higher ratio in terms of sales above those for general SMEs (Kim, 2007).

SMEs in the 2010s: win–win growth policy

In recent years, the policy focus of the government for SMEs has been placed on the promotion of a 'win–win growth strategy' and support between large companies and SMEs in various sectors. The government initiated various business-friendly policies and implemented plans for fostering 50,000 zero innovative SMEs, creating 500,000 jobs, simplifying SME start-up procedures, expanding a public purchasing system and strengthening financial support through various deregulations. The need for win–win growth policy between large companies and SMEs was stressed to ensure the sustainable competitiveness of SMEs in the global marketplace. To this end, the Korean Commission for Corporate Partnership was founded in 2010, and Measures to Implement Win–Win Growth Policy between Large Companies and SMEs were announced in September of 2010. The win–win growth strategies included the establishment of a fair-trading order, SME business area protection, spreading of win–win growth strategy and support for strengthening of SMEs' autonomy. Although the government intended the win–win growth strategy to go hand in hand between large companies and SMEs, the policy achievement was considered insufficient so far. Also, the government intended to focus on the funding support at an initial stage of SME to overcome the financial crisis and focused on regulations to solve an issue of bipolarization in growth between SMEs and large companies (Lee, 2011).

Structural and qualitative changes in policy for Korean SMEs

A low ratio of medium-sized firms playing a bridging role between large companies and SMEs may often result in a concern for the weakening of the overall industrial structure and excessive industrial concentration can be a problem. As noted above, after the financial crisis in 1997, the number of SMEs in Korea continuously increased (e.g. 19.8%), while the number of large companies continuously declined (e.g. 28.9%). Also, in the small and medium-sized manufacturing industry, the ratio of heavy and chemical industry continued to increase fast, compared to the ratio of the light industry. It is also noted that while the light industry ratio had declined in all sectors, for example, in the number of companies, the number of employees and output in the heavy and chemical industry ratio increased annually, surpassing 70% in terms of output in 2005 (see Figure 3 below).

Also, the ratio of Korea's light industry and heavy and chemical industry is about 3:7, while the ratio of the U.S. and/or Japan is about 4:6. As such, the heavy and chemical

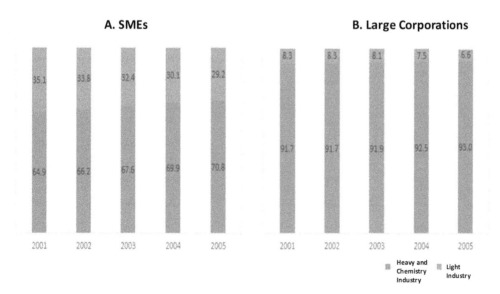

Figure 3. Heavy and chemical industry ratio for SMEs and large corporations.

Table 3. Production ratios of major countries by industry (unit: %) (KEB Economic Institute 2004).

Category	Korea		U.S.		Japan	
	1980	2003	1980	2003	1990	2003
Light industry	47.2	29.4	52.8	39.4	45.4	46.8
Heavy and chemical industry	52.8	70.6	47.2	60.6	54.6	53.2

Source: Statistics Korea, 'Statistics Survey Report of Mining and Manufacturing Industries', Each issue of US Census Bureau, 'Quarterly Financial Report', Japanese Ministry of Finance, 'Monthly Statistical Report of Finance and Banking'.

industry ratio in Korea is at a very high level compared to those of other developed countries (Table 3 below). One thing to note here is that the light industry ratios of developed countries appear to remain at a certain level, which may mean that there might exist some SME-unique light industry sectors in Korea (KBIZ, 2010), despite the country's industrial progress.

Over the years, as global competition increases, Korea's labor-intensive industry has been losing its competitiveness, and a large portion of Korea's labor-intensive industry has moved to China or other developing countries in which labor costs are cheaper (Statistics Korea, 2005). However, production activities seem to remain at a sufficient level in Korea based on product gentrification and differentiation, and technology innovation. The increase of Korean heavy and chemical industry ratio has both positive and negative aspects. This may also imply that the production competence that was concentrated on labor-intensive industries quickly moves to capital-intensive industries. For example, by comparing major export items in the 1990s, mid-1990s and 2000s, one can speculate that SMEs production competence shifted over time from labor-intensive industries to the capital-intensive industries. Namely, as shown in Table 4, in the 1990s, the order of export items changed from textile and electricals and electronics in 1990 to

Table 4. Change of Korean SMEs' export items.

Ranking	1st	2nd	3rd	4th	5th
1970	Textile	Machinery	Commodity products	Furniture	Daily supplies
1975	Textile	Machinery	Commodity products	Chemical products	Daily supplies
1980	Textile	Machinery	Commodity products	Chemical products	Daily products
1986	Textile	Machinery	Commodity products	Chemical products	Daily products
1990	Textile	Electricals and electronics	Daily supplies	Machinery, Transporting machines	Commodity products
1995	Electricals and electronics	Textile	Machinery, Transporting machines	Plastics, rubber, leather products	Steel, metal products
2000	Electricals and electronics	Textile	Machinery, Transporting machines	Plastics, rubber, leather products	Steel, metal products
2003	Electricals and electronics	Machinery	Textile	Chemical industrial products	Steel, metal products
2004	Electricals and electronics	Machinery	Textile	Chemical industrial products	Steel, metal products
2005	Electricals and electronics	Machinery	Textile	Chemical industrial products	Steel, metal products
2006	Electricals and electronics	Machinery	Chemical industrial products	Textile	Steel, metal products
2007	Electricals and electronics	Machinery	Chemical industrial products	Steel, metal products	Textile

Source: KBIZ (Korea Federation of Small and Medium Business).

Table 5. Trends in Korean innovative SMEs (unit: companies).

Category	2001	2002	2003	2004	2005	2006
Venture business	11,392	8778	7702	7967	9732	12,216
Inno-Biz	1090	1856	2375	2762	3454	7183
Management innovative company	–	–	–	–	–	2619
Innovative company (excluding duplicity)	11,783	9500	8558	8839	10,731	17,512

Source: KBIZ (Korea Federation of Small and Medium Business).

the order of electricals and electronics and textile in 1995, and then in the 2000s into the order of electricals and electronics, machinery and textile in 2003 (KBIZ, 2010).

This also supports a view that the advent of the innovative SMEs in the 2000s showed a possibility that small scale companies can grow in a high added value markets, if they are equipped with technological prowess and innovation capability. By way of example, innovative SMEs including venture/start-up businesses and other innovation focused businesses (such as Inno-Biz companies and management innovative firms) increased substantially in number from 11,783 in 2001 to 17,512 in 2006 (Table 5 below). According to the SMBA, in 2007 the number of innovative SMEs was 24,719, venture businesses was 14,015, Inno-Biz companies was 11,526 and management innovative companies was 6510 (KBIZ, 2010; Korea Federation of Small and Medium Business (KBIZ); Korea Federation of SMEs, 2008, 12).

Challenge and outlook relating to SME limitations

Generally, one of the objectives of national policy for SMEs is to address problems that SMEs face in the marketplace. Sometimes, there may be a structural problem that is disadvantageous to SMEs but with change to national policy, such a situation can be altered. This is because a large proportion of the problems that SMEs face is often related to economic or industrial problems which are derived from or rooted in economic and industrial environmental conditions. However, the economic and industrial policies employed to solve these economic and industrial environmental conditions may unwittingly make SMEs more difficult to thrive in the changing environments. Also, certain policies that are designed for SMEs may be difficult to execute if they are to solve an SME's difficulties only. Furthermore, even if the policies are executed effectively, the effects of the policies may be very limited in scope (Yeom, 2007).

Sometimes, the challenge that SMEs face is a megatrend of economic environment change, which may include mid- and long-term factors affecting market demand and supply functions. Such megatrends may comprise different constraints on production factors such as the intensification and tighter integration of the global economy, acceleration of technological innovation and new technology fusion, aging of population structure, lack of resources or broader environmental problems. Looking at the intensification and tighter integration of global economy, it is easy to note that the speed of internationalization or globalization has accelerated quickly since the 1990s with the advent and development of information and communications technology, as well as the integration of socialist countries (including Eastern Europe and China) into the market economy system, financial liberalization and deregulation on capital movement. These are some of the challenges that SMEs in Korea may have to deal with in the coming years.

In recent years, the Korean national economy has experienced many transfers of production facilities to developing countries where manufacturing costs are more favorable than in Korea. In years to come, the transfer of production bases to these developing countries is expected to continue with a higher frequency on a global scale. As this trend continues, the technology-intensive and knowledge-based industries will tend to be concentrated in the developed countries as they have relatively better trained labor resources and technological development infrastructure. The Korean economy is no exception to this expected future trend.

Also, the Korean national economy is presently experiencing what is called a 'nutcracker situation' in that Korea is positioned between the developed countries with advance technology and the developing countries with certain competitive advantages such as very low labor costs, production costs, etc. in the marketplace. That is, Korea's technology level is at par with that of the developed countries in many areas, but Korea is experiencing certain losses in the competitiveness in production costs, compared to the developing countries, such as China and Vietnam. However, in view of this, Korea's comparative advantages may be used as a leverage against the developing countries such as China and Vietnam. The nutcracker situation may be overcome through active transformation of its national economy to a high-tech and high added value industry structure, as Korea advances in the new technology sector beyond what has been accomplished so far. For SMEs in Korea, this may mean that the SMEs need to actively embrace and implement their innovation strategy in such a way that they shift from technology innovation based on traditional production factors (e.g. labor and capital) to technology innovation based on new information and knowledge (Yu, 2007).

Policy vision for Korean SMEs

In the new economic environment characterized by a knowledge-based economy and limitless competition on a global scale, SMEs in Korea need to emerge anew as a unit of innovation. Namely, in the face of the new economic environment, the new role of SMEs is to create high quality employment opportunities and produce high-added value rather than mass produced products. This means that more than ever SMEs need to play a leading role in changing the industrial structure and becoming a new driving force for the growth of the Korean national economy for the future. This role may be viewed as being beyond their conventional role in the past, which is often characterized as contributing to the creation of employment in a simple national economy, diffusing competition based on specialization, and creating quality employment opportunities. Further, to be in line with SMEs' new role, a future policy for SMEs needs to lay out ways for the strengthening of SMEs' core competencies (with innovation competency as one of the foremost policy goals).

For building the innovation competency of SMEs, three core tasks must be strongly promoted and carried out for SMEs: (1) change in technology financing/distribution function; (2) establishment of innovation system(s) and (3) enhancement to human resources structure. Further, support for SMEs' technology development and improvement, as well as the development of overseas markets for SMEs' products and/or services, needs to be provided to help bolster and maintain the competitive advantages of SMEs in Korea. Also, from a policy standpoint, in addition to SMEs' active technology development in collaboration with middle standing companies and multinational corporations, there is an on-going need to actively transform SMEs into global companies (e.g. global suppliers for parts and materials industries). To strengthen the competitiveness of SMEs, joint negotiation capability may be built and fostered through building an assembly of networks to achieve various competitive advantages that cannot be enjoyed at an individual SME level. To survive in the twenty-first century's global business environment, the realization of the strengthened global competency has become an urgent task for many SMEs in Korea, which may require additional help based on changes in the policy vision for SMEs.

Conclusions

In recent years, the Korean economy has posted the highest growth rate among Asia's high growth countries (Choi, 2013), which was made possible based on the economic restructuring efforts established by government-led policies for enterprises and/or companies over the past five decades. Although Korea suffered several set-backs due to severe economic crises, including two instances of oil shock and foreign exchange crisis during its economic growth process, the Korean national economy rebounded each time, making a track record of remarkable recovery. As the government policy for SMEs has been continuously adapted and implemented, the contribution of SMEs to Korea's national economic development has become significantly higher, resulting in big gains for the policy makers for SMEs in Korea. Also, it is noted that the opening of the Korean market and changes in the comparative advantage structure resulted in that the SME sector has experienced numerous structural changes, in addition to numerous changes in the manufacturing sector, advancement of the post-industrialization in Korea, and increase in the scope of the service industry.

The government policy for SMEs in Korea was created within the development process of the country's modern capitalism. The core of existing government policy aims to solve and ease the problems of SMEs. As such, the government policies for SMEs in Korea should be established in a way to better deal with the SMEs' problems such as a manpower shortage and win–win growth issues with large companies. The future of Korean SMEs will depend upon each SME's desire and determination for bringing innovations into the global marketplace. This will require changes in technology, financing/distribution function, establishment of innovation systems, and the enhancement of the labor structure, together with win–win growth strategy between large companies and SMEs in Korea.

Acknowledgements

This paper is based on materials prepared by The Presidential Commission on Small and Medium Enterprises, The Republic of Korea, in which one of the authors participated. In particular, this paper is mostly based on the 2007 report by The Presidential Commission on Small and Medium Enterprises, The Republic of Korea.

Disclosure statement

No potential conflict of interest was reported by the authors.

Funding

This work was supported by the Catholic University of Korea Research Fund, 2016.

References

Choi, H. G. (2007). Future of Korean economy and SMEs. *Future of Korea Economy and SMEs*. Special Contributions on Policy Direction for SMEs. The Presidential Commission on Small and Medium Enterprises, Republic of Korea.

Choi, S. G. (2013). *Policy outlook and assessment to Korean SME Policy in the Past 10 Years*. Seoul: Korea Small Business Institute.

Heo, B. D. (2007). Mid-term policy need to be focused on global competitiveness enhancement. *Future of Korean Economy and SMEs*. Special Contributions on Policy Direction for SMEs. The Presidential Commission on Small and Medium Enterprises, Republic of Korea.

KBIZ. (2007). The survey results of venture business 2007.

KBIZ. (2010). International small business statistics 2007.

KEB Economic Institute. (2004). Statistics of major Countries relating to SMEs.

Kim, G. M. (2007). Making hidden winners. *Future of Korean Economy and SMEs*. Special Contributions on Policy Direction for SMEs. The Presidential Commission on Small and Medium Enterprises, Republic of Korea.

Korea Federation of Small and Medium Business (KBIZ). International Small Business Statistics 1992–2010.

Korea Federation of SMEs. (2008, 12). International small business statistics.

Korea National Statistical Office. (2005). Survey Report on Business Statistics 2005.

Lee, B. G. (2011). *Economic policy shaping and Lee Myung Bak administration's policy evaluation and advancement tasks*. Seoul: Korea Economic Research Institute.

Lee, J. W. (2006). *A study on the systematic managerial support for each step of growing phases of small and medium size enterprises*. Seoul: Graduate School of Business Administration, A-jou University.

Lee, K. U. (2014a). *History of Korean SMEs*. Seoul: Jisic-Sanup.

Lee, K. U. (2014b). *Korea SME's business theory*. Seoul: Jisic-Sanup.

Seo, J. D. (2014). *Small businesses: Development, current situation and priorities for the future*. Seoul, Korea: Korea University Press.

The Presidential Commission on Small and Medium Enterprises. (2007). *Future of Korean Economy and SMEs*. Seoul: The Presidential Commission on Small and Medium Enterprises, Republic of Korea.

Statistics Korea. (2005). Report on statistics of mining and manufacturing industries 2005.

Yeom, H. C. (2007). Harmony between efficiency and equity. Special Contribution on Policy Direction for SMEs. *Future of Korean Economy and SMEs*. Special Contributions on Policy Direction for SMEs. The Presidential Commission on Small and Medium Enterprises, Republic of Korea.

Yu, G. H. (2007). Painful top three policy tasks for SMEs. *Future of Korean Economy and SMEs*. Special Contributions on Policy Direction for SMEs. The Presidential Commission on Small and Medium Enterprises, Republic of Korea.

The financing of new firms: what governments need to know[*]

David Storey and Julian Frankish

ABSTRACT
Governments in all OECD countries either currently have, or have previously had, publicly funded programmes to improve access to finance amongst new and/or small firms. This paper provides insights to governments on the risks associated with funding such businesses. It shines a light into this opaque marketplace by examining the survival and default records of more than 6000 new business clients with Barclays Bank over 10 years. It finds approximately one-in-four start-ups that receive finance will experience a default at some point in their life-cycle and concludes there are significant risks for governments seeking to intervene in this marketplace.

Introduction

Governments in all OECD countries either currently have, or have previously had, publicly funded programmes to improve access to finance amongst new and/or small firms (Hussain & Scott, 2015; OECD, 2007). There are both economic and social rationales for such funding. The economic rationale is that the finance market for new and smaller firms exhibits two failures. The first is that, because of their size, they are disadvantaged in obtaining access – at least in comparison with larger firms (Roberts, 2015). The availability of finance to new and small firms is said to be opaque because these firms lack a sufficient track record on which their risk can be adequately assessed, with many also lacking the necessary collateral to support higher value lending. This opacity means (some) 'good' firms may be denied access to funding (Berger & Udell, 2002; Cressy, 2002) while others may not seek finance in the first instance because they expect to be rejected (Kon & Storey, 2003). The second potential failure around access to finance is that the social returns from funding new and small businesses could be significantly higher than private returns. This is often cited as a key reason for supporting firms identified as being innovative, particularly where the development of such innovation requires substantial upfront investment. In such cases these firms may be unable to access finance because of imperfect knowledge about the scale of investment needed to bring an innovation to a market ready state and the scale of demand even when it has reached that point. In both cases the inability of 'good' new and small firms to

---

[*]Julian Frankish writes in a personal capacity and the views expressed do not necessarily reflect the views of Barclays Bank.

81

access funding (enabling them to survive and grow) represents a loss for the rest of society in forgone output, employment and tax revenues.

The social case for funding is based on the argument that entrepreneurship can be an exit route from disadvantage for both owners and the employees of these businesses (Frankish, Roberts, Coad, & Storey, 2014). This disadvantage may be based on gender, race or other personal characteristics (Cho & Honorati, 2014; Cooney, 2014) or more broadly on the geographic location of the business, its owner and employee base. The provision of public funding to individuals unable to raise personal or commercial finance enables them to start and grow businesses, thus increasing the chances of them exiting from deprivation, which in turn has knock-on benefits for society and the economy. Whilst public funding can have these highly desirable consequences it is important for governments to also be aware of the risks involved (most notably that new and small firms have a considerably higher risk of closure than larger firms). A convenient 'rule of thumb' provided by Hart and Oulton (1998) is that for companies with up to 500 employees, each doubling in size, reduces closure rates by 5%.[1] Therefore, the risk is that public funds only stimulate and support the creation of short lived businesses, with minimal impact on aggregate output and employment.

This paper seeks to provide insights to governments on the risks associated with funding both new and small businesses. It seeks to shine a light into this relatively opaque marketplace by examining the characteristics of new start-ups and draws important distinctions that are relevant for policy-makers. The first is to identify the characteristics of new start-ups that obtain funding from a formal source (in this case Barclays Bank in the UK) and to compare them with otherwise similar new firms that do not seek or do not obtain funding. The second contribution of the paper is to distinguish (among those that secure funding) between those that default and those that do not. Its core finding is that about one-in-four new start-ups which obtained funding from the bank defaulted at some point in either their whole lifespan or their initial 10 years. It also shows that there are clear patterns amongst those that default, with this being much more likely in the early years of trading and amongst the smaller firms. However, even with these patterns and a strong commercial incentive, it is apparent that assessing short-to-medium term default risk to a high degree of accuracy is extremely challenging.

This poses a problem for governments which will be discussed in more detail at the end of the paper. The problem is that governments in high income countries are keenly aware that when significant numbers of viable new and small firms are unable to access funding, there is a knock-on effect on economic output, employment and tax revenue. On the other hand, both direct and indirect financial support carries the risk of encouraging economically and socially inefficient levels of start-up and small business activity. In short, how does public policy ensure that 'good' businesses receive finance while limiting the number of 'bad' recipients? This paper suggests that there are three policy options open to government. The first is to provide funding for SMEs directly; the second is to engage-with, or partner, the formal financial institutions in making joint lending decisions some of which are underpinned by public funds. The third option is to see access to finance as a market-failure problem and seek to make the new and small firm marketplace more competitive – without making any direct or indirect use of public funds.

Prior work and issues

The scale of public funding to support new and small firms (particularly in developed countries) is rarely documented but when calculated the sums are considerable. The UK was the first government in the world to conduct an estimate of the scale of taxpayer support for both enterprise policy and SME policy (DTI, 2003; National Audit Office [NAO], 2006). The central finding of the Department of Trade and Industry (DTI) review was that aggregate expenditure was approximately £8–10 billion a year. As a benchmark, at that time expenditure on policing and universities were both slightly lower, at approximately £7 billion a year. A more recent review by Lundstrom et al. (2014) for Sweden showed that their spending was approximate to the UK on a per-capita basis. Such funding is frequently justified on the grounds of market failure, most notably due to imperfect information. Hussain and Scott (2015) note that small firms in general, and start-ups particularly, are at a disadvantage compared with larger, longer established firms, both in accessing the funding necessary for them to start trading, and to subsequently sustain and grow those businesses. Numerous reasons are put forward to support this position. The first is that the survival rates of such new/small businesses are lower and hence, from the viewpoint of the lender, they are riskier. The second disadvantage is that although some new/small firms are potentially low risk, it can be difficult or impossible for them to credibly signal this to lenders in the absence of a visible track record. Consequently, there is a strong likelihood that some 'good' businesses will be rejected for funding, thereby limiting their growth potential and imposing a loss both upon them and the rest of the economy and society. Thirdly, because 'good' businesses are rejected, some new and small firms that (in a fully informed marketplace) would have sought funding but instead do not apply and are often referred to as 'discouraged' borrowers (Kon & Storey, 2003).

The justification for public intervention in the provision of finance to new and small firms is therefore that the opaque nature of the market causes a loss to society because 'good' businesses are prevented from accessing funds to enable them to start-up, survive and subsequently create jobs and wealth. To address this governments in many countries have introduced a range of credit guarantee programmes[2] which exhibit considerable diversity, but also have several common features. The first is that they involve some form of underwriting of the loan by the government. This is intended to provide a degree of loan security to lenders and thus allow some additional firms to obtain debt finance that they would not otherwise be able to access on commercial terms. The second is that there is an interest rate premium on the loan that is used to cover some (or all) of the costs of both operating the guarantee programme and meeting the higher risks associated with such finance.

As noted earlier, in other cases public funding for new and small firms is restricted to certain 'types' of individuals or businesses. The most widely supported 'types' are new and small firms in the high-technology sectors. The largest-scale example is the Small Business Innovation Research (SBIR) programme in the United States, where total public funding has exceeded $2 billion (Link & Scott, 2009). In other cases, the focus is on the location of the business, its owners and/or its employees. Direct and indirect public financial support for new and small firms is considerable, particularly in high and middle-income countries. It is also clear that given their scale, it is important to assess the risks associated with such activities, most notably by a study of the default rates experienced by commercial lenders over an extended period. Only by carefully analysing the actual experience of such lenders can governments assess the likely level of public funding that must be committed to ensure an improvement in access to funds for new and small businesses.

Barclays data: sample, definitions and 'representativeness'

To explore the issues around finance use by start-up businesses, the research draws upon a large sample of such firms that has previously served to examine survival and growth over an extended period (Coad, Frankish, Roberts, & Storey, 2013). The data are taken from the records of Barclays Bank, a significant provider of financial services to the UK business population. Each business in the sample was a start-up with Barclays between March and May 2004. By this it is meant the enterprise opened its first designated business current account in this period and had income enter this account (credit turnover) by the end of the following month. In addition to this basic requirement, some other restrictions were placed on the initial pool of start-ups to arrive at the final sample. First, they had to be either a company, partnership or a sole trader. Second, they had to be engaged in non-financial activity. Third, they needed to have answered some voluntary questions covering educational attainment, prior business experience and the use of business advice before start-up.

With the above conditions in place, the initial sample comprised around one-in-four of all start-ups with Barclays during the three-month period considered.[3] These new businesses were subsequently tracked over the following 10 years, with the sample adjusted to account for the switching of some firms to other banking providers and more accurately assigning the closure dates of others. Taking these changes into account, a sample of 6579 start-ups was attained whose survival and performance could be followed over a decade. It is important to emphasise that:

> The sample comprises those enterprises newly provided with current account facilities. It is not restricted to those seeking or obtaining financial services such as loans or overdrafts. Since (virtually) all businesses in the UK require access to a bank account, the sample closely reflects the composition of UK start-ups during this period, without having the disadvantage of the official business register where those included are either: (1) above a (high) sales threshold or (2) within the payroll tax system.

As set out below, about one-in-four start-ups used finance from Barclays within their first 12 months of trading, implying that the vast bulk use either their own resources or no resources during that time.[4] The purpose of this paper is to examine the characteristics of the 25% of start-ups using Bank finance (but recalling that they are different from the full sample). Another key advantage of using bank data is the ability to supplement it with additional variables for some considerable period after the sample was originally constructed. In this case, when seeking to examine finance use in more detail, researchers could back-populate additional data on: (1) finance use, and (2) default events. The paper will draw upon these data in the next section.

Defining finance use

The measure of 'finance use' applied is whether the start-up held an overdraft limit and/or a term loan *with Barclays* during each 12-month period following start-up that they remained active. The emphasis is to make clear that these data do not represent a comprehensive view of external finance use within this sample. However, additional survey derived analysis means that researchers are confident that they account for the (vast) majority of such use. More than 90% of UK SMEs only hold a business current account with their 'main bank'. Given that the presence of an overdraft limit is dependent on this type of account, this paper will be observing almost all such use. Similarly, around 90% of SMEs with term loans obtain them from the same bank in which they have their current account. Taking these points together leads one to conclude that the data represents a robust view of finance use across these start-ups. It is important to emphasise that the data does not capture those firms in the sample that applied for finance within a given period *and whose applications were declined.* The incidence of finance rejection is an important area for study, but not one that is not addressed in this paper.

Defining default

Two items are used to define a 'default event'. The first is that a start-up has a 'non-performing' marker placed on one (or more) of their accounts, representing a material incidence of lending arrears. The second is that they have an account moved to a 'recovery unit'. This represents a more overt assessment of default as it is a key step on the path to Barclays' seeking to formally recover outstanding lending. These measures are considered because the use of a marker does not necessarily lead to a subsequent formal recovery as the lending may be unsecured or of sufficiently low value to be deemed uneconomic to pursue.

While this paper is concerned with the incidence of default among finance users, it should be noted that it is possible for businesses without sanctioned finance use to be recorded as in default. This will occur when businesses without an overdraft limit have an 'unauthorised' overdraft balance for a protracted length of time.

Results

Start-ups: survival

Table 1 below provides a summary of the survival and closure profiles of the study's 6579 start-ups over the decade from 2004 to 2014 taken from Coad, Frankish, Roberts, and Storey (2016). Of the initial firms, only 1208 (18%) remained active after 10 years. Closure rates were highest in Years 2 and 3, with more than one-half exiting the business stock in the first 36 months. This rate then declines in subsequent years. This temporal pattern is broadly akin to that found in several previous studies[5] (Headd, 2003). Table 1 also shows the size (measured by credit turnover) of these start-ups. At the end of Year 1, the mean income of surviving firms was £114,000, although one-half had sales of less than £40,000. Perhaps of greater significance is that sales growth over time is neither consistent throughout the sample, nor over time. For example, Table 1 shows that the median level of firm income falls in three of the 10 years, and when the increases are positive, only in Year 2 do they exceed 5%. The overall impression of the sample is one of high exit rates and low growth rates, but with a tiny minority achieving very fast growth.

Table 1. Summary statistics for size and growth rates.

	Mean sales	SD	10%	25%	Median	75%	90%	Obs
Year 1	114,095	508,678	5475	14,687	38,712	103,658	260,652	5524
Year 2	144,319	546,146	5547	16,529	44,524	124,414	323,178	4162
Year 3	168,352	645,409	5222	17,253	47,855	138,347	373,255	3211
Year 4	183,939	542,018	5438	18,532	51,964	158,026	428,499	2593
Year 5	190,217	552,839	5945	17,996	51,168	152,264	451,445	2152
Year 6	192,157	706,588	5239	17,517	47,924	147,866	453,727	1823
Year 7	213,050	938,730	5700	18,475	53,019	161,941	512,618	1604
Year 8	253,250	1,333,538	6668	19,516	58,134	177,112	577,178	1424
Year 9	277,643	1,640,798	6533	19,274	57,258	180,390	595,597	1311
Year 10	300,699	2,046,271	6860	22,673	64,989	196,821	592,880	1208
	Mean sales growth	SD	10%	25%	Median	75%	90%	Obs
Year 1	–	–	–	–	–	–	–	–
Year 2	−0.055	0.940	−0.964	−0.270	0.053	0.356	0.753	4162
Year 3	−0.133	0.946	−1.001	−0.303	0.022	0.240	0.566	3211
Year 4	−0.110	0.864	−0.873	−0.280	0.013	0.226	0.503	2593
Year 5	−0.189	0.907	−0.991	−0.378	−0.067	0.135	0.427	2152
Year 6	−0.221	0.833	−0.864	−0.368	−0.080	0.086	0.359	1823
Year 7	−0.089	0.772	−0.696	−0.207	0.005	0.185	0.475	1604
Year 8	−0.055	0.698	−0.593	−0.198	0.000	0.184	0.458	1424
Year 9	−0.078	0.731	−0.592	−0.222	−0.022	0.147	0.436	1311
Year 10	−0.037	0.678	−0.518	−0.175	0.020	0.203	0.484	1208

Note: There are 6579 firms at the start of Year 1.
Source: Coad et al. (2016).

This must be borne in mind when examining the use of bank finance and the resulting default rates.

Who uses bank finance?

This section presents the scale of finance use within the sample and how this varied by business characteristics. Figure 1 shows that just over one-third (36%) of start-ups used bank finance *in any year* over the decade covered by the sample. However, that proportion varied considerably as the cohort aged. In their first year (which can be regarded as the 'at

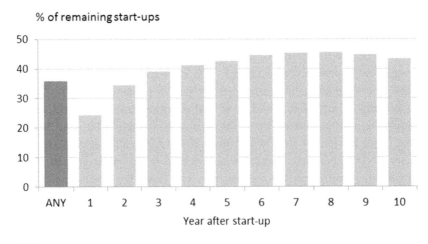

Figure 1. Finance use.

start' time for this purpose), only about one-in-four start-ups used Bank finance. As the cohort matured, this proportion steadily increased to a peak of 45% of surviving firms in Year 8.

However interpreting Figure 1 does require care. The first proviso is one mentioned in the previous section – namely it shows those in receipt of bank finance, not those who sought funding and were declined. Nor is it known how many were discouraged from seeking funds. Second, as shown in Table 1, the sample size falls over time as businesses close. So although the proportion of (surviving) firms in receipt of finance rises, this is strongly influenced by the exit of firms that are not financed by the Bank. This is highlighted in Coad et al. (2016) who show that closing businesses were typically poorer performing in the immediately preceding period and were therefore less likely to have been provided with bank finance. Therefore, part of the rise observed in Figure 1 reflects changes in the composition and scale of the denominator.

The research shows that comparatively few start-ups make the transition to using bank finance once the business matures. Figure 2 shows that more than 80% of those with any finance use did so initially within their first two years and more than 90% within three years. Given that there was significant attrition of the sample in these initial years, it is perhaps unsurprising that first use was also heavily concentrated in the same 36 months. However, the conditional probability of first finance use (i.e. in the next 12 months given that the firm has reached a certain age) can also be examined. As can be seen in Figure 2, this likelihood drops off very sharply after the first couple of years and by the time the (remaining) cohort are seven years old, less than 2% of 'never users' will become users within the next year.

While these data are unadjusted for business characteristics, they do suggest that finance use may not just be the result of a carefully considered choice about whether it is likely to benefit the firm at a specific point in time, but also it reflects past experiences. Therefore, a relatively established business that has never used external finance appears unlikely to do so because it would represent a step change in what has been (until then at least) a successful or satisfactory trading model.

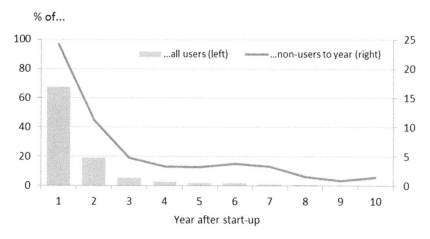

Figure 2. Finance use, first time.

A second set of factors influencing the use of bank finance were the size and industry of the start-up. Figure 3 shows the striking relationship of use with the maximum size of the start-ups while trading (or the 10 years, if they survived the full period). For the smallest, only around one-in-five saw any finance use, with this proportion rising to 70% where (maximum) turnover exceeded £1 m. This probably reflects that smaller firms can operate effectively without material levels of stock or other assets beyond those provided by internal sources.

Figure 4 shows the industrial distribution of finance use. It varied from more than 40% of relevant firms in retail, transport and manufacturing to less than 30% for real estate, professional and information activities. These differences probably link to typical levels of tangible assets and may also reflect contrasting size distributions.

A third group of factors show that finance use is not only associated with direct business characteristics, but can also reflect those of firm owners. One example of this, shown in Figure 5, is that use rises and falls with owner age, peaking at 40% for those aged 35–44 (at start-up), but is below 30% for the under 25s and amongst those of retirement age.

Another example (not shown) is that finance use was notably higher where owners had prior business experience, compared with those without such a background. Both this and the differences may be attributable to factors such as differing levels of resources (financial and skills), plus contrasting ambitions for the start-up. One interpretation is that for many of the over 65s, bank funding is not sought because the business has limited growth aspirations and because the limited funding required can come from personal assets. For those under the age of 25, a rather different explanation is likely. It is well-established (Cressy, 1996) that new businesses established by young people have considerably higher closure rates than those established by middle-aged individuals. This is likely to be reflected in the risk assessments made by potential lenders, with the lower rate reflecting both higher decline rates and greater discouragement among these owners.

A final area of variation in finance use relates to the legal form of the start-up. Prior work has shown it to influence both business survival and growth (Cassar, 2004; Cressy, 1996). Cressy (1996) showed that limited company start-ups were significantly

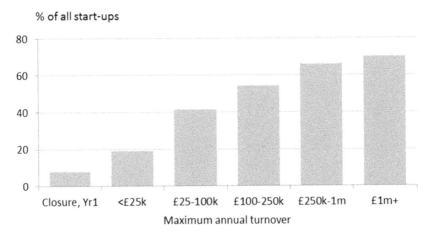

Figure 3. Finance use, firm size.

% of all start-ups

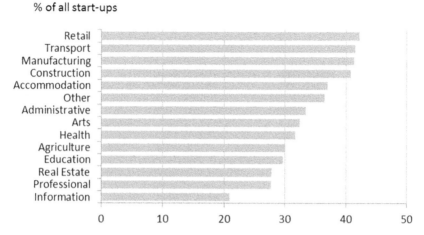

Figure 4. Finance use, industry.

more likely to survive and grow than those that chose to be sole traders or partnerships. Figure 6 does indeed show that the finance use of sole traders was relatively low, although the difference with other legal forms was relatively modest. However, the sample also identifies that finance use by partnerships exceeded that for companies.[6] Further, the data reveal that finance use was more likely amongst those start-ups with 'additional' owners,[7] perhaps indicating that risk assessments implicitly or explicitly weigh-up the additional resources brought to the business by a greater number of owners.

Who defaults?

Finance providers tend to pay special attention to discrete periods, typically 12 months, whether considering default expectations or the development of actual default outcomes. The analysis will consider these, but before doing so it is worth examining the aggregate

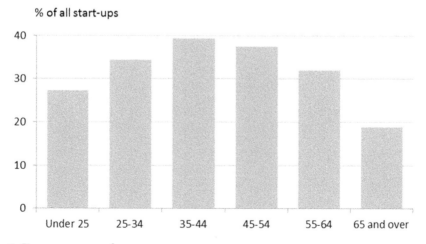

Figure 5. Finance use, age of owner.

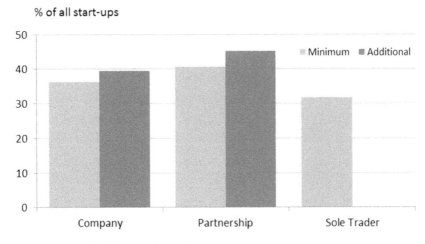

Figure 6. Finance use, legal form and number of owners.

default picture across the whole sample for the full 10 years available. The headline figure is that more than one-in-four start-ups (27%) who had bank finance experienced default at some point.[8] This may appear to represent a very high incidence of default, but it is the outcome of (in most cases) multiple years of such finance use. The consideration of default over an extended period offers a noticeably different perspective than more regular 12 month views.

Figure 7 sets out more conventional default rates (the proportion of finance users in a specific year defaulting in that year) for the decade covered by the sample. It shows that default rates rose sharply after start-up, reaching more than 7% of relevant businesses in Years 2 and 3, before starting on a broad downward path for the remainder of the period to a low of 2% in Year 10.

The period covered by Year 1 of the sample is Spring 2004 to Spring 2005. In turn, Year 4 corresponds to 2008–2009, which was during the depth of the UK recession. Given this, it is interesting that there appears to have been only a limited increase in default rates

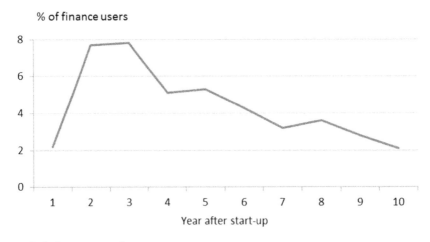

Figure 7. Default rate, annual.

among finance users, albeit that the true impact measure should probably be how far they were above the 'expected' default rate in that year (i.e. given regular trading conditions). Even allowing for this, the slowing economy in the first half of 2012 (Year 8) seems to have had a more marked effect than the earlier more dramatic downturn.

The absence of a clear association between default rates and broader economic conditions may have been due to fluctuations in relatively small sample sizes (e.g. there were 65 defaults across 1250 finance users in Year 4). However, it may also say something about the weak link between macro-economic variables and defaults on small lending balances. These can often display a 'random' pattern, even when higher value lending follows a more clearly explicable path. Looking again at Figure 7, it is striking that the default rate profile looks similar in shape (if not level) to overall business closure rates shown in Figure 1. This raises the question of the relationship between these two measures. The sample indicates that defaults translate into closures within a relatively short time. Over the 10 years nearly 90% of defaulting firms closed in the same 12-month period as the default was recorded in. If one also allows for those instances where defaults and closures fell either side of the boundary between two periods, then the link is even stronger. Indeed, among the sample, only one start-up was recorded as defaulting on more than one occasion. Examining this relationship from the other direction reveals broad stability over time, with around one-in-five closures in any year being associated with a default. This highlights that although business closure may be the result of not meeting income objectives, the majority are not linked to financial 'distress'.

Default rates, business characteristics

This section examines how long-term default rates (the incidence of default across the whole of our dataset) varied by business characteristics. This approach is used to maximise the sample sizes available in the study. Figure 8 shows that long-term default rates declined with the maximum size of the start-up, going from 30% for the smallest firms to 16% for those where turnover exceeded £1 m. However, it is also apparent that the difference in default rates was relatively modest (about five percentage points) across many finance

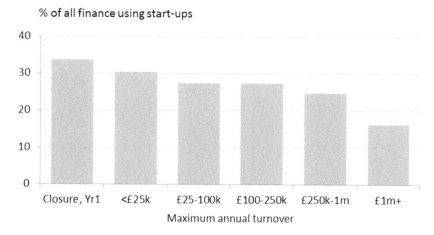

Figure 8. Long-term default rate, firm size.

% of all financing using start-ups

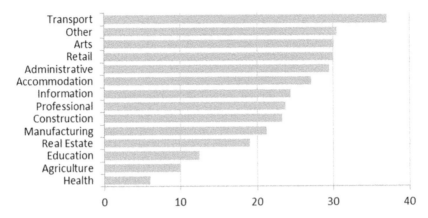

Figure 9. Long-term default rate, industry.

users, with only the largest size category being significantly different. This may reflect the risk assessment process applied by the bank before making finance available (i.e. only applicants above a given risk threshold will be accepted), with the result that subsequent default outcomes are compressed.

Figure 9 shows the wide range of default rates seen across industries, from less than 10% to more than 40%. While some of this variation may be the result of stochastic factors acting on modest sample sizes, it is unlikely to be a coincidence that the lowest rates are in three sectors that might be expected to have relatively consistent income flows from year-to-year – health, agriculture and education. In each case these are closely associated with public spending or transfers, while agricultural firms typically have high levels of tangible assets relative to their size.

Figure 10 shows that there was a marked contrast in default rates between companies and sole traders on the one hand and partnerships on the other. This may have been due to

% of all finance using start-ups

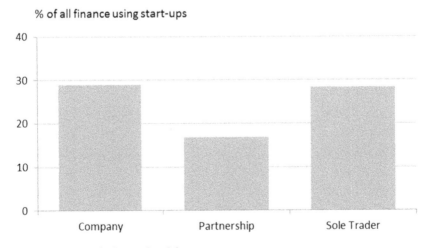

Figure 10. Long-term default rate, legal form.

the concentration of partnerships in certain industry groups or differences in the type of owners choosing this legal form. However, it could also be linked to the unlimited liability of partnerships and more particularly the fact that this would impact on someone else (unlike the position for sole traders). This may make partnerships more conservative than businesses using other legal forms.

Regardless of the exact cause, the pattern of default rates across legal forms is worthy of further investigation due to the contrast with closure rates. Both in this dataset and other studies (Coad et al., 2016), companies have lower closure rates. Taken together these results could imply that banks have tended to 'over-lend' to limited companies or that business owners judge that banks favour limited companies, leading to a greater use of this legal form than would otherwise be the case.

Figure 11 shows the association between default rates and the age of business owners. For those under 45 at the date of start-up default rates were around 30%, with only modest variation from the youngest to the oldest in this age range. In marked contrast, the default rates for those aged 45–64 were 10 percentage points lower at 20% over the long-term. Part of this difference may be down to the business composition of these two broad age groups, including measured factors such as prior business experience, but also other elements not captured by the dataset such as the personal resources available at and after start-up. Another possibility is that, as discussed above for partnerships, owners in this age range may have lower risk preferences.

Finally, among broader owner characteristics, one interesting result shown in Figure 12 is the higher default rates for owners with low educational attainment and those with the highest levels. The former may be a proxy for initial and subsequent resources, together with financial management, while the latter may suggest a link between greater business ambitions and heightened risk.

Conclusions

As was noted at the introduction to this paper, access to finance is widely seen to be a key factor influencing the creation of new firms, their survival and longer term performance.

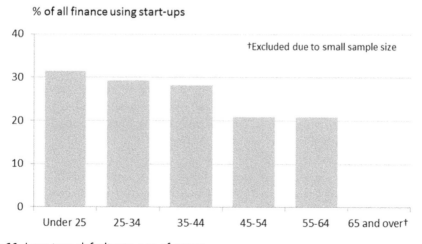

Figure 11. Long-term default rate, age of owner.

% of all finance using start-ups

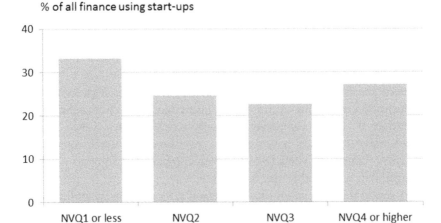

Figure 12. Long-term default rate, owner education.

For these reasons, public policies in all developed economies have sought to enhance the provision of external finance to them on the basis that such support enhances both output and employment over the medium-to-long term. The challenge facing governments is to provide financial support in ways that do not result in either excessive cost or a large amount of deadweight. There have been a range of approaches seeking to balance improved access and control costs and undesirable incentives. One is the creation of state-funded loan guarantee programmes (Cowling & Siepel, 2013) which underwrite loans made by specified financial institutions to new and small firms. In some countries, the scale of these programmes is considerable. For example, in Mexico public support in 2011 for the national guarantee system exceeded $250 m (OECD, 2013, p. 98).

An approach that has been pursued in the UK for some years is the commitment to improve the diversity of supply in small business finance by introducing measures to reduce the role of the main banks. This effort to make the SME finance market more 'competitive' has taken different forms. They include the support given to the so-called challenger banks, consisting of both established, but smaller providers, and new entrants. This has gone alongside policies to reduce the barriers for SMEs switching between banks (both for finance and wider banking needs[9]), to increase the data available to all suppliers on small business and to place declined lending applications in front of alternative providers.

In addition to direct government action, broader technology changes in financial systems are producing developments with the potential to enhance access to finance. Perhaps the most widely discussed of these is the rise of peer-to-peer (P2P) or marketplace lending, using IT to match potential lenders (individuals, businesses and other financial service providers) with firms seeking external finance. The attraction for borrowers is not usually lower cost lending, but a quicker application and acceptance process. In the UK, the largest of the business P2P lenders, Funding Circle provided £600 m in 2015.

The challenge facing governments is to balance what are referred to as Type I and Type II errors. A Type I error is when a 'good' SME (i.e. one that would have repaid the funds lent to it) is rejected for finance, thus imposing the loss on society of the economic activity that would have been generated had such a loan been provided. The Type II error is when a loan is made and the SME defaults which results in losses to the bank, other creditors and other parties. This weighs particularly heavily on loan finance where there is no 'upside' (as is the case for equity). Both types are also likely to have second-round effects in reducing the likelihood of applicants coming forward and the acceptance of those who do.

The study makes it clear that Type II errors are material, even with the incentives facing a commercial lender and their accumulated experience in observing the characteristics of those that have defaulted in the past. A rough rule-of-thumb is that approximately one-in-four start-ups that receive finance will experience a default at some point in their life-cycle. It suggests that, although there are patterns in the characteristics of those new and small firms that default, it is currently not possible with a high degree of accuracy to reject applications for funding from such firms. It is for this reason that the performance of the P2P lenders will be watched with interest as macro-economic conditions change.

What has to be recognised is that taxpayer-backed funding for new and small firms will focus on the (even) more risky segment of the SME financial marketplace than that covered by commercial lenders. It therefore moves lending up the risk curve and must be expected to have rates of default, perhaps considerably, higher than is the norm for commercial banks. The UK experience of Loan Guarantee programmes[10] is that default rates on loans, with a life of up to 5 years, were 40% for start-ups.

Governments, acting on behalf of taxpayers, therefore need to be aware of the potential scale of losses of such programmes. As a minimum they need to publicly articulate, in advance of the programme becoming operational, what degree of additional risk is acceptable and why. Furthermore those responsible for delivering such funding to enterprises have to be made aware, before the programme starts, that it will be the subject of continuous robust evaluation, based on clearly specified objectives and targets.

Finally, we ask the reader to consider whether such funding actually helps the borrowers. In the UK there is a clear cost of default to the business owner and to its creditors. For these reasons it is reasonable to ask whether public funds should be used to encourage excessive 'ambition' that may increase the already high risk of default, with downside consequences for all parties. In short, are 'socially' driven loan programmes that see nearly one-half of recipients in arrears, the best way of helping those individuals?

Notes

1. Companies with 1 or less employees have a 2 year death rate of 48%; those with up to 4 employees have a rate of 40%; those with 5–8 employees have a 31% rate; those with 16–32 employees have a 26% rate; those with 64 to 128 have a 15% rates, etc. Only beyond 256 employees is there no consistent relationship between death and size rates. Table 2, p. 13 Hart and Oulton (1998).
2. A recent review found that variants of such Schemes operated in 54 countries (Samujh, Twiname, & Reutemann, 2012).
3. It is important to note that finance use among this start-up sample may not be representative of that for all new firms from 2004. Additional analysis indicates that the usage levels were somewhat higher than for other start-ups from the same three month window. This may be due to a degree of self-selection introduced by only including those who answered the voluntary questions mentioned earlier.
4. This proportion appears almost invariant over time. For example, in a survey of new businesses in North East England found the proportion using banks was 25% in 1979 and 23% in 1990 (Storey & Strange, 1993).

5. Headd (2003) shows that 66% of new employers survive two years or more, 50% survive four years or more, and 40% survive six years or more.
6. It is worth noting that early 2004 was at the end of a two year period when there had been an unintended tax incentive that made incorporation look particularly attractive. This may have skewed the type of business within each legal form, that is, more companies that were 'effectively' sole traders.
7. In excess of the minimum required for that legal form, that is, company 2+, partnership 3+.
8. We must be clear that this does not represent the losses to the bank on their lending as this will be related to the interest and capital repayments received prior to default and the proportion of any funds that can be recovered from a defaulting business, so called 'loss given default'.
9. In 2013 small businesses became able to use a switching mechanism that guaranteed the transfer of a current account, including all direct debits and standing orders, within seven working days, rather than several weeks.
10. Graham (2004), Chart 3.13, page 27.

Disclosure statement

No potential conflict of interest was reported by the authors.

References

Berger, A. N., & Udell, G. F. (2002). Small business credit availability and relationship lending: The importance of bank organisational structure. *The Economic Journal, 112*(477), F32–F53.
Cassar, G. (2004). The financing of business start-ups. *Journal of Business Venturing, 19*(2), 261–283.
Cho, Y., & Honorati, M. (2014). Entrepreneurship programs in developing countries: A meta regression analysis. *Labour Economics, 28*, 110–130.
Coad, A., Frankish, J. S., Roberts, R. G., & Storey, D. J. (2013). Growth paths and survival chances: An application of Gambler's ruin theory. *Journal of Business Venturing, 28*(5), 615–632.
Coad, A., Frankish, J. S., Roberts, R. G., & Storey, D. J. (2016). Predicting new venture survival and growth: Does the fog lift? *Small Business Economics, 47*(1), 217–241.
Cooney, T. (2014). Offering minority communities equal opportunities through entrepreneurship. *Ciencias Económicas, 10*(2), 73–86.
Cowling, M., & Siepel, J. (2013). Public intervention in UK small firm credit markets: Value-for-money or waste of scarce resources? *Technovation, 33*(8–9), 265–275.
Cressy, R. C. (1996). Are business startups debt-rationed? *The Economic Journal, 106*(438), 1253–1270.
Cressy, R. C. (2002). Introduction: Funding gaps: A symposium. *The Economic Journal, 112*(477), F1–F16.
Department of Trade and Industry (DTI). (2003). *Cross cutting review of government services for small business*. London: Author.
Frankish, J. F., Roberts, R. G., Coad, A., & Storey, D. J. (2014). Is entrepreneurship a route out of deprivation? *Regional Studies, 48*(6), 1090–1107.
Graham. (2004). *Graham review of the small firms Loan guarantee. Interim report*. London: HM Treasury.
Hart, P. E., & Oulton, N. (1998). *Job creation and destruction in the corporate sector: The relative importance of births, deaths and survivors* (Discussion Paper No 134). London: National Institute of Economic and Social Research.
Headd, B. (2003). Redefining business success: Distinguishing between closure and failure. *Small Business Economics, 21*(1), 51–61.
Hussain, J. G., & Scott, J. M. (2015). *Research handbook on entrepreneurial finance*. Cheltenham: Elgar.

Kon, Y., & Storey, D. J. (2003). A theory of discouraged borrowers. *Small Business Economics*, *21*(1), 37–49.

Link, A., and Scott, J. T. (2009). Private investor participation and commercialization rates for government-sponsored research and development: Would a prediction market improve the performance of the SBIR programme? *Economica*, *76*(302), 264–281.

Lundström, A., Vikström, P., Fink, M., Meuleman, M., Głodek, P., Storey, D. J., & Kroksgård, A. (2014). Measuring the costs and coverage of SME and entrepreneurship policy: A pioneering study entrepreneurship. *Theory and Practice*, *38*(4), 941–957.

NAO. (2006, May 24). *Supporting small businesses*. Report by the comptroller and auditor general. London: National Audit Office.

OECD. (2007). *Framework for the evaluation of SME and entrepreneurship policies and programmes*. Paris: Author.

OECD. (2013). *Mexico: Key issues and policies* (OECD Studies on SMEs and Entrepreneurship). Paris: Author.

Roberts, R. (2015). *Finance for small and entrepreneurial business* (Routledge-ISBE Masters in Entrepreneurship). Abingdon: Routledge.

Samujh, R.-H., Twiname, L., & Reutemann, J. (2012). Credit guarantee schemes supporting small enterprise development: A review. *Asian Journal of Business and Accounting*, *5*(2), 21–40.

Storey, D. J., & Strange, A. (1993). *Entrepreneurship in Cleveland, 1979–1989: A study of the effects of the enterprise culture*. London: Employment Department Research Series No 3.

Government agencies should be exemplars of business behaviour

Mark Allsop and Mark Brennan

ABSTRACT

Australian business leaders informed the development of a framework that outlined their views of what model business behaviours are and how these can be driven through appropriate business action. This framework overviews that organisations who seek model business behaviour should:
- Establish a clear direction and robust strategy
- Develop and sustain relationships with stakeholder
- Put people first and engage with staff
- Measure outcomes and evaluate success

Further consultation with Australian government leaders highlighted that these model behaviours could largely be adopted by Australian government agencies when they operate as a business. Application of these behaviours would help drive exemplar business behaviour more broadly.

Introduction

The purpose of this paper is to comment on the proposition that government agencies, in their commercial dealings, should behave in an exemplary manner. Whilst there is no reason in principle why this proposition should not extend to all government agencies, in the context of work undertaken to date, the focus of this paper is on Commonwealth Government agencies (Department of Finance, 2013).[1] Further, research to which this paper relates is derived by reference to the reports and materials considered, which, in the main, were also composed by the authors of this paper.

The proposition that Commonwealth Government agencies should be exemplars of business behaviour is related to observations made by the Australian Small Business Commissioner on how improvements can be made to the quality of the business environment, by all participants, in effect, 'lifting their game' (Australian Small Business Commissioner, 2015). These observations were informed over a decade of experience of the concept of a Small Business Commissioner, firstly in Victoria and then in other State jurisdictions and at the national level.

Business-to-business report

The initial interest in business behaviour was taken by the Victorian Small Business Commissioner. A flagship function of Small Business Commissioners is facilitating the resolution of disputes. In 2007, the Victorian Small Business Commissioner identified that improvements in the facilitation of business-to-business disputes could be made if there were improvements in business behaviour. The subsequent report identified seven behaviours that can be characterised as instructive to establishing and sustaining successful business relationships. Briefly stated these are:

- *Alignment* with businesses that share the same values;
- *Commitment* to treat each relationship as a long-term arrangement based on trust;
- *Mutual Interest* of each business to achieve a common goal of a profitable, sustainable and on-going relationship;
- *Communication* must be clear, transparent, frequent and at the right level;
- *Accountable and Responsible* agreeing to obligations and responsibilities and immediately alerting business partners of any problem or mistake;
- *Professional Conduct* in all interactions;
- *Pre-agreed Dispute Resolution* is essential so that any disagreements can be dealt with quickly and the relationship can continue with minimum disruption. (Victorian Small Business Commissioner, 2007)

To a considerable extent, this first report into business-to-business behaviour paved the way for a similar examination of government-to-business behaviour. Again, observations made through the experience of Small Business Commissioners prompted the initiative to examine the participation of government agencies in the business world.

Study of model business

It was apparent to the Australian Small Business Commissioner that it was worthwhile exploring the way in which government agencies should behave when participating in commercial dealings. In this regard, it is not necessarily front of mind for government agencies to perceive themselves as significant participants in business. A clear enough exception though is in the area of procurement where it is very obvious to government agencies that they are heavily involved in business transactions when undertaking procurement activities. Whilst procurement is a prominent business activity for government agencies, there are other examples of government agencies participating in business activities, such as:

- supplying services, including in partnership with private sector businesses;
- administering government programmes beneficial to business;
- acting as a landlord in respect of government-owned property and
- as a tenant in private sector-owned property.

This range of business activities demonstrated to the Australian Small Business Commissioner that there was scope for government leadership in the Australian business community. Just as the Victorian Small Business Commissioner had sought to improve the quality of the business environment by seeking to identify exemplary behaviour in business-to-business dealings, so it seemed to the Australian Small Business Commissioner that government agencies should be an exemplar of behaviour in their business dealings.

The expectation that government agencies should be exemplars is not unfamiliar to Commonwealth Government agencies. In Australia, when engaged in litigation, Commonwealth Government agencies are expected to behave as model litigants (Office of Parliamentary Counsel, 2005). Similarly, when Commonwealth Government agencies are engaged in business activities, it is not unreasonable to expect them to behave as model businesses. Having decided that there is a sound rationale for Commonwealth Government agencies to be exemplars of business behaviour, the Australian Small Business Commissioner undertook a project to identify the characteristics of a model business operating within Australia and to establish how these characteristics can be adopted or adapted by Commonwealth Government agencies. The Office of the Australian Small Business Commissioner appointed Deloitte Private (Deloitte) to engage with Commonwealth Government agency leaders to understand how Commonwealth Government agencies, in their interactions with business, can and should behave as a 'model' business.

This project initially entailed the Australian Small Business Commissioner and Deloitte engaging with Australian business leaders to answer a key question – 'In 2014, what are model business behaviours and what are the outcomes that result from acting as a model or exemplar business?' The resultant study produced a model business framework and recommended testing with Commonwealth Government leaders whether the framework could be adopted, or needed to be adapted, for potential application across Commonwealth Government agencies (Australian Small Business Commissioner, 2014b). Underpinning the model business framework was the assumption that compliance with the law was a fundamental model behaviour. Key findings of the initial phase of the project established four 'model' business commitments and a set of leadership traits, organisational values, principles and practices that exemplify 'model' business behaviour. Australian business leaders expect that a business should commit to:

- establish a clear direction and robust strategy;
- develop and sustain relationships with stakeholders;
- put people first and engage with its staff and
- measure outcomes and evaluate success.

The expectations of Australian business leaders formed the basis of a model business framework, the details of which are contained in Table 1 prepared by the study.

Report on government agencies as model businesses

The second phase of the project was to consult with senior leaders from Commonwealth Government agencies, in the context of the business leaders' study, and to draft a report (Australian Small Business Commissioner, 2014b). The report concluded that the fundamentals of 'model' business behaviour are the same, regardless of private or public sector. Specifically, for the public sector, leaders of Commonwealth Government agencies are

Table 1. Model business framework for Australian businesses.

	Establish a clear direction and robust STRATEGY	Develop and sustain relationships with STAKEHOLDERS	Put people first and engage with STAFF	Measure outcomes and evaluate SUCCESS
Leaders are	1. Courageous and able to communicate a vision 2. In touch and conscious of current and future operating environment 3. Forward thinking and confident in challenging status quo	1. Customer-driven and connected with broader industry eco-system 2. Reasonable, fair and practical in negotiation 3. Aware of conflicting interests and the importance of compliance	1. Consultative and constructive when building consensus 2. Attentive and supportive of staff development needs 3. Open-minded and embracing of diversity	1. Focused on performance, excellence and risk 2. Plain spoken and direct in communicating results 3. Prudent and objective when responding to a crisis
Values signal a culture that is	1. Purposeful 2. Agile 3. Innovative	1. Empathetic 2. Consistent 3. Responsible	1. Collaborative 2. Capable 3. Inclusive	1. Effective 2. Transparent 3. Accountable
Principles guide everyone to	1. Operate by a clear vision and charter 2. Sense, respond and deliver value to the market 3. Exercise creativity and make defensible decisions	1. Understand needs of all parties – customers, suppliers, partners 2. Articulate a position and agree goals that deliver mutual benefit 3. Meet obligations and act ethically and early to resolve disputes	1. Demonstrate a collegiate and respectful work ethic 2. Pursue opportunities for professional growth 3. Celebrate difference and appreciate work/life balance	1. Operate efficiently without compromising quality 2. Report achievements regularly based on value not process 3. Identify, own and learn from failures
Outcomes	1. Instill confidence in ability to achieve goals 2. Achieve and sustain a point of difference in the market 3. Allocate and apply resources efficiently and effectively	1. Sustain valuable and repeatable business transactions 2. Realise mutual benefit from a 'win/win' situation 3. Avoid costly and damaging disputes	1. Achieve high levels of productivity and enthusiasm 2. Attract and retain good and reliable people 3. Cement a unique brand as an 'employer of choice'	1. Grow sustainably and in line with expectations 2. Achieve a commercial, social and environmental return 3. Augment reputation as an industry and market leader

recognised as having the responsibility of first driving recognition among staff of the role of the agency as a business and secondly educating and engaging with businesses about this role and expected 'model' behaviours. The report noted that any differences from public sector to private businesses, where they exist, should be clearly explained and understood but should not result in a materially different set of 'model' behaviours.

As with the Australian business leader study, consultations with Australian government leaders proceeded on the assumption that a fundamental of model business conduct is compliance with the law and focused on identifying model business actions and activities for participants in the Australian business environment. The report developed a 'model' business framework specific to Commonwealth Government agencies for their potential

Table 2. 'Model' business behaviour framework for government agencies.

	Establish a clear business intent and robust STRATEGY	Form and maintain relationships with STAKEHOLDERS	Put people first and engage with STAFF	Measure outcomes and communicate SUCCESS
Leaders are	1. Courageous and able to communicate a vision 2. In touch and conscious of current and future operating environment 3. Forward thinking and enquiring in challenging status quo	1. Able to work in partnership with leaders from all sectors 2. Reasonable, fair and practical in negotiation 3. Aware of conflicting interests and the importance of compliance	1. Consultative and constructive when building consensus 2. Attentive and accessible to staff and their needs 3. Open-minded and embracing of diversity	1. Focused on performance, excellence and risk 2. Plain spoken and direct in communicating outcomes 3. Prudent and objective when responding to a crisis
Values Signal A Culture That Is	1. Purposeful 2. Adaptable 3. Innovative	1. Empathetic 2. Impartial 3. Responsible	1. Collaborative 2. Capable 3. Inclusive	1. Effective 2. Transparent 3. Accountable
Principles Guide Everyone To	1. Operate by a clear vision and charter 2. Seek out and consider opportunities to improve 3. Exercise creativity and make defensible decisions	1. Understand and respect different views and values 2. Act impartially however work in partnership to agree and achieve shared goals 3. Meet legal and professional obligations; act ethically and early to resolve disputes	1. Demonstrate a collegiate and respectful work ethic 2. Pursue opportunities for professional growth and career development 3. Celebrate difference and appreciate work/life balance	1. Operate efficiently without compromising quality 2. Report performance based on outcomes not process 3. Balance a tolerance of risk with the responsible achievement of outcomes
Outcomes	1. Provide a confidence in meeting business objectives and government priorities 2. Strengthen ability to respond and adapt to change 3. Allocate limited resources efficiently and effectively	1. Provide opportunities to engage in effective government to business partnerships 2. Realise mutual benefit whilst maintaining a level playing field 3. Avoid costly and damaging disputes	1. Achieve high levels of productivity, commitment and enthusiasm 2. Attract and retain people with similar values but a breadth of experience and skills 3. Reinforce a brand as a public sector 'employer of choice'	1. Achieve business objectives, organisational outcomes and government of the day priorities 2. Protect public interest whilst interacting with the business community 3. Augment a reputation as an effective business within the Australian public sector

application. A copy of the 'model' business behaviour framework for government agencies prepared by the report is set out in Table 2.

The report found that Commonwealth Government leaders believe that there is significant alignment between expected 'model' business behaviour from both the public and private sector – with limited adjustment required to be made to the 'model' business framework to make it applicable for government agencies. Commonwealth Government leaders contend that the aspiration to meet the four 'model' business commitments – strategy, stakeholders, staff and success – is as important to a government agency as it is to a business:

- A leader is accountable for how well an organisation is meeting its legislated responsibilities and 'model' business commitments. The breadth of experience, perspective and personal values of a leader is considered significant in determining the extent to which a government agency acts as a 'model' business.
- The value by which an organisation operates indicate to staff and stakeholders how business is to be conducted. Values establish a cultural expectation of behaviour and should be reflected in all business practices. For government agencies, the values that symbolise a 'model' business culture should complement the Australian public service values and principles. (Australian Public Services Commission, 2016)

Many of the leadership principles underlying 'model' business behaviour are considered to be equally relevant to both government agencies and businesses. There is however some adjustment required to account for the need for government agencies to:

- balance the priorities of the government of the day with individual organisational responsibilities;
- operate within the public sector accountability and transparency framework;
- 'Strive to maintain a level playing field' with fairness and equity in its market engagement and
- deliver public value and outcomes that are in the public interest.

The report contends that an exemplar business is viewed as one that prioritises the need to educate its stakeholders about differences in motives, obligations or process and engage on how these can be incorporated into a business relationship.

The report found that there is a consensus of Commonwealth Government leaders that when a government agency behaves as an exemplar business it will produce outcomes that benefit the agency and businesses with whom they have a direct relationship. However, the example set by the agency will also play a vital role in reinforcing a standard of conduct that, if adopted by all agencies and businesses, will lead to a more effective and efficient business environment benefiting all participants in the Australian economy. When setting its corporate strategy, a government agency considers its objectives for all its operating responsibilities, including instances where it acts as a business. By reflecting its business purpose in a clear statement and proposed actions, a government agency is able to:

- provide confidence in meeting business objectives and government priorities;
- strengthen the ability to respond and adapt to change and
- allocate limited resources efficiently and effectively.

Public service accountabilities that are particular to government agencies impose specific business engagement processes and protocols that need to be followed. When building a relationship with any stakeholder, it is the responsibility of government agencies to educate about why these processes exist and seek solutions about how the impost can be minimised. By seeking out and establishing business relationships, government agencies are able to:

- access opportunities to engage in effective government to business partnerships;
- realise mutual benefit whilst maintaining a level playing field and
- avoid costly and damaging disputes.

Recruiting and retaining the right staff is critical to being able to operate successfully and perform at a standard that meets or exceeds Australian public service standards and expectations. Highly engaged staff generally outperform those less engaged, enabling a government agency to:

- achieve high levels of productivity, commitment and enthusiasm;
- attract and retain people with similar values but a breadth of experience and skills and
- reinforce a brand as a public sector 'employer of choice'.

Commonwealth Government agencies are concerned with how they can operate productively and effectively to deliver the priorities of the government of the day whilst looking for opportunities to innovate and improve practices into the future. When government agencies look to actively measure their outcomes and communicate their success, they are able to strengthen their ability to:

- achieve business objectives, organisational outcomes and the priorities of the government of the day, sustainably;
- protect public interest whilst interacting with the business community and
- augment a reputation as an effective business within the Australian public sector.

The report developed six recommendations to support the development of model business behaviours, which are summarised as follows:

(1) Strategy: plan for a model business culture.
(2) Stakeholders: engage with business to educate and clarify expectations of model business behaviour.
(3) Stakeholders: be responsive to the needs of businesses.
(4) Stakeholders: reflect on different types of business relationships (i.e. customers, supplier, landlord, etc.) and responsibilities.
(5) Staff: encourage staff to challenge and provide feedback about how model business behaviour can be adopted.
(6) Success: take stock of achievement of business outcomes.

Whilst these recommendations were generated within the context of Australia, they are applicable to government agencies across the globe.

Benefits and practicalities of government model business behaviour

It is arguable that the report gives rise to a certain expectation on small and large businesses to adopt 'model' commercial practices when contracting other businesses. As such, it is reasonable and fair for government agencies, in their business activities, to also adopt 'model' business behaviours and be an exemplar to other government agencies as well as the business community. If government agencies are an exemplar of 'model' business behaviour, they will play a role in influencing all participants in the business community to act in a similar manner. The outcome of which will be contributing to 'raising the bar' of Australian business standards – improving the overall quality and productivity of the business environment. The benefits for which will flow to Australian businesses, particularly small business (Australian Small Business Commissioner, 2015).

In terms of practical implementation, a critical success factor for the adoption of 'model' business behaviours by Australian government agencies is identifying what they are, and then building key stakeholder support for their adoption. In this practical sense, there appears to be scope in the areas of contracting and subcontracting for Commonwealth Government agencies to demonstrate leadership in business behaviour. A report by the Australian Small Business Commissioner in 2013 into underpayment and contracting issues relating to the construction of the ASIO building in Canberra is instructive as to a pivotal role that Commonwealth Government agencies can play in business transactions. In this matter, a major issue was transfer of risk and responsibilities ultimately on to small business subcontractors. Although a major focus of the report concerned the relationship of the big business contractor, engaged by a Commonwealth Government agency, with small business subcontractors, the report does make recommendations about improved Government contracting processes and management on large Commonwealth construction projects. In the context of model business behaviour, the ASIO Building report contains an interesting commentary:

> There is a view by government agencies that the most efficient use of taxpayer funds when it comes to large projects is to appoint a managing contractor, who is subsequently responsible for the tendering of all trade packages on the project. As there is not a contractual relationship with the subcontractors, the agency takes an 'arm's length' approach in respect of the relationship with, and payment of, the subcontractors. Any disputes between the contractor and subcontractors then become a 'commercial contractual matter' and not the responsibility of the agency.

> While on most accounts engaging a private sector contractor would be the most appropriate and efficient approach to manage large projects, we do not believe that this should completely absolve the agency of all responsibility for robust project management. When government agencies are behaving as a business, it is the view of this office that they have an obligation to act as a 'model business' to influence industry behaviour positively, setting best practice standards, being a good corporate citizen and demanding similar behaviour from its suppliers, even when this may come at an additional cost. (Australian Small Business Commissioner, 2014a)

The ASIO Building report elevates the model business aspiration to that of an obligation, similar to the model litigant obligation, for Commonwealth Government agencies. Moreover, the ASIO Building report, in effect, suggests that there are positive duties in model business behaviour to influence behaviour of other businesses and demand model business behaviours from them.

The aspiration that Commonwealth Government agencies should behave as a model business is a worthy one. The pursuit of a public sector culture of model business behaviour would benefit from a strategy of education. Further, there appears to be scope for useful work to be done in developing meaningful performance indicators of model business behaviour.

Note

1. Government agency is defined as any Commonwealth Department, Commonwealth entity or Commonwealth company that is subject to the Public Governance, Performance and Accountability Act 2013 (Department of Finance, 2013).

Acknowledgements

The authors appreciate assistance with respect to the preparation of this paper and the related reports and study provided to them by Gemma Cooper and Claire Szatsznajder.

Disclosure statement

No potential conflict of interest was reported by the authors.

References

Australian Public Services Commission. (2016). *APS values and code of conduct in practice*. Canberra: Australian Government. Retrieved from http://www.apsc.gov.au/publications-and-media/current-publications/aps-values-and-code-of-conduct-in-practice

Australian Small Business Commissioner. (2014a). *ASIO building: The cost of poor contracting practices*. Canberra: Australian Government. Retrieved from http://www.asbc.gov.au/sites/default/files/ASBC_Business_behaviours_WEB_NEW.pdf

Australian Small Business Commissioner. (2014b). *Australian business leaders: A study of model business behaviours*. Canberra: Australian Government. Retrieved from http://www.asbc.gov.au/sites/default/files/ASBC_Business_behaviours_WEB_NEW.pdf

Australian Small Business Commissioner. (2015). *Government agencies behaving as model businesses*. Canberra: Australian Government. Retrieved from http://www.asbc.gov.au/sites/default/files/ASBC_Business_behaviours_WEB_NEW.pdf

Department of Finance. (2013). *Public governance, performance and accountability act 2013*. Canberra: Australian Government.

Office of Parliamentary Counsel. (2005). *Legal services directions 2005: Appendix B*. Canberra: Australian Government.

Victorian Small Business Commissioner. (2007). *Forming and maintaining winning business relationships*. Melbourne: Office of the Small Business Commissioner. Retrieved from www.vsbc.vic.gov.au/news-publication/business-conduct-report/

Colombia small- and medium-sized enterprise's 70 years of progress: what's next?

Rodrigo Otoniel Varela Villegas

ABSTRACT

A detailed review is made of the micro, small and medium sized enterprise policies that had been proposed and implemented in Colombia in the last 70 years. It is a descriptive review without evaluations of the impact of each one of the policies. The article ends with the main policies that are in effect in 2016.

Introduction

When policy-makers from any country gather together to determine what enterprise policies they should introduce to support small business, few people outside of government appreciate the enormous challenges that they face. For example, they must decide whether the objective of their policies is to have more (i.e. new) firms or 'better' (sustainability or growth) firms, plus they must decide whether they will deliver the new initiatives through Micro or Macro policies. There are also multiple other considerations involved such as whether they should target-specific industry sectors, whether the initiative should be nationally or regionally based, and what budget can be allocated to the initiative. The policy-makers also know that it is extremely difficult to measure the effectiveness of the initiative because they are so many variable factors (some measurable, some not) that can impact upon the outcome of an initiative. Additionally, they will be aware that the population expects them to get the decision correct every time. The OECD Framework is a very useful tool to enable policy-makers to visualize the array of possibilities that they might consider introducing to enhance small business activity in their country (Figure 1).

Profile of Colombia

Colombia is a country of approximately 48.2 million people, located in the north-western corner of South America with an approximate land area of 1,142,000 km^2. Despite a troubled recent history, it has been developing its social and economic dynamics with positive results. Its GDP per capita adjusted for purchasing power parity (GDPPC PPP) has been growing at an average annual rate of 2.9% over the past 20 years. In 1992, its GDP per capita was $4791 dollars per capita but by

Determinants						Entrepreneurial performance	Impact
Regulatory Framework	Market conditions	Access to finance	Knowledge creation and diffusion	Entrepreneurial capabilities	Culture	Firm based	Job creation
Administrative burdens for entry	Anti-trust-laws	Access to debt financing	R&D investment	Training and experience of entrepreneurs	Risk attitude in society	Employment based	Economic growth
Administrative burdens for growth	Competition	Business angels	University/industry interface	Business and entrepreneurship education (skills)	Attitudes towards entrepreneurs	Wealth	Poverty reduction
Bankruptcy regulations	Access to the domestic market	Access to VC	Technological co-operation between firms	Entrepreneurship infrastructure	Desire for business ownership		Formalizing the informal sector
Safety, health and environmental regulations	Access to foreign markets	Access to other types of equity	Technology diffusion	Immigration	Entrepreneurship education (mindset)		
Product regulation	Degree of public involvement	Stock markets	Broadband access				
Labour market regulation	Public procurement	**Firms**		**Employment**		**Wealth**	
Court and legal framework		Employer enterprise birth rates		Share of high growth firms (by employment)		Share of high growth firms (by turnover)	
Social and health security		Employer Enterprise death rates		Share of gazelles (employment)		Share of gazelles (by turnover)	
Income taxes: wealth/bequest taxes		Business churn		Ownership rate start-ups		Value added, young or small firms	
		Net business population growth		Ownership rates business population		Productivity contribution, young or small firms	
		Survival rates at 3 and 5 years		Employment in 3 and 5 year old firms		Innovation performance, young or small firms	
Business and capital taxes	Patent system; standards	Proportion of 3 and 5 year old firms		Average firm size after 3 and 5 years		Export performance, young or small firms	

Figure 1. OECD framework. Source: OECD (2014).

2012 it was $10,583 dollars. This growth was boosted by the development of the mining and hydrocarbon sectors, and by the evolution of financial services. In 2012, the Colombian economy was in 28th place in the world when measured by GDP. Since 2012, due to the fall of oil and mineral prices, the Colombian economy has been greatly affected. Processes that had occurred in the previous ten years, such as the revaluation of the Colombian peso in relation to the US dollar, have been reversed and now a devaluation is in progress. This change will undoubtedly negatively affect the results of the GDP per capita in dollars, although it will improve the export possibilities for Colombian companies (Reina, Castro, & Tamayo, 2013). The Colombian situation regarding unemployment has been improving since 1995, but it remains close to 10% (with a 50% informal sector). Another factor that hinders the Colombian development is that the investment in research and development remains as one of the lowest in Latin America (0.15% of GDP in 2010). Colombia has shown a reduction of 20% in poverty rates, but it still has relatively high levels when compared to other countries in the region such as Brazil, Chile and Mexico (Reina et al., 2013). In 2012, Colombia was ranked: 60th in the Global Innovation Index, 69th in the Global Competitiveness Index; 55th in the PISA Reading, 58th in the PISA Science and 61st in the PISA Math, 93rd in infrastructure, 109th in institutional quality, and 87th in human capital and research (Reina et al., 2013). Between 2015 and 2016, Colombia fell from 52nd to 54th in the World Bank 'Doing Business Report' (World Bank, 2016).

Historical development

Although Colombian business processes, in the SME sector (small- and medium-sized enterprises, including micro-enterprises), are as old as the pre-Columbian cultures that practised commercial, agricultural, mining and production activities using barter as the main economical mechanism, the sector as such only became recognized by academics, unions and governments in the late 1940s. On the other hand, there were 'craft guilds' from the eighteenth century, but the first association of entrepreneurs in the SME sector was generated in 1952 with the creation of ACOPI (Asociación Colombiana de Pequeñas Industrias, n.d.). This guild emerged as a private initiative of entrepreneurs, supported by membership fees. It sought to defend the State law of democracy with its own entrepreneurial and politic initiatives, and to identify solutions for small Colombian companies. Over the past 70 years, numerous adjustments were made to policies that support SMEs, many programmes and projects were implemented, the objectives and scope of the guilds have been set-up and changed, many supporting organizations have been created as well, and several laws have been issued. For that reason, it would be interesting to review some of these initiatives from a historical perspective.

In 1940, the Colombian Government created the Institute of Industrial Development (IFI, Instituto de Fomento Industrial) to support its industrial development. The IFI was the state-financed instrument responsible for promoting the foundation, expansion or merging of basic production units and processing enterprises. It also had responsibility for responding to the provisions on credit democratization contained in the development plans of different governments. Its establishment was justified by the lack of the private sector's interest in financial activities and the need to generate a financial scheme for the industrial sector in an economic model based on import substitution. This decision provided financial backing with medium and long-term credits for enterprises. In 1945, Colombia made the first census of manufacturers and found that there were 7853 establishments employing more than five and less than 99 employees. These numbers translated into 135,400 direct jobs between administrative employees and labourers, and these were concentrated in five departments: Antioquia, Atlántico, Cundinamarca, Santander and Valle del Cauca (Garay, n.d.).

In 1950, the national government founded the Banco Popular with the aim of providing credit to SMEs. The Banco Popular managed to gather unionization initiatives that had taken place in various cities, giving birth to ACOPI in January 1952, with the following main objectives:

(1) Represent and defend the Colombian entrepreneurs' interests, especially those of the SME sector,
(2) Work for the development of domestic credit finance,
(3) Submit to the authorities the needs and aspirations of the enterprises, asking them to secure, to modify or to derogate laws and provisions related to their enterprises,
(4) Manage with the relevant authorities the application of a duty scheme that will effectively protect local companies from foreign competitors.

The alliance between ACOPI and Banco Popular partially helped to solve the credit problems of SMEs. ACOPI launched two major development projects: the creation of an organization with the ability to organize international fairs and exhibitions (CORFERIAS) and the creation of industrial parks and neighbourhoods where business centres could settle.

In 1952, ACOPI presented its 12-point economic plan, which highlighted the following issues (Asociación Colombiana de Pequeñas Industrias, n.d.):

- Adjustment of the role of the Industrial Development Institute (IFI)
- Development of long-term credit
- Cultivate favourable tariffs to protect domestic industry
- Encourage the export orientation of SMEs
- Review tax policies so that taxes would be charged relevant to industry size
- Development of differential rates in public services relevant to company size
- Establishment of technical assistance programmes
- Create industrial schools
- Encourage compensation trade pacts with other countries
- Guidelines for the participation of foreign capital in Colombian industry

In 1952, the first permanent exhibition of small industry was held in Bogotá with the participation of 300 small businesses, and ACOPI also organized the first industrial mission to Europe to identify options that could help improve the Colombian industry (Pallares, 2002). In 1953, a new manufacturing survey was conducted with ISIC methodology, and they found that in Colombia there were 11,243 establishments with more than 5 and less than 99 employees, demonstrating the rapid growth of this sector in the Colombian economy in the late 1940s and early 1950s. Additionally, big multinationals came to Colombia and started some integration processes between SMEs and large enterprises (Pallares, 2002). In 1954, the first international industrial fair was held with the participation of 20 countries. It was the first industrial fair in Latin America. In Cali, ACOPI not only commenced the development of the ACOPI Industrial Zone by building factories, but it also oversaw the construction of housing facilities for employees of those industries. In the following years and under a protectionist tariff policy, established in the 1950s, Colombian SMEs enjoyed significant growth as indicated by the data in Table 1 below.

When the political problems that disrupted the Colombian democratic tradition were solved, ACOPI presented to the national government (1958–1962) several proposals to help the development of the MSME sector:

- Create a stabilization fund to guarantee investments of small industrialists
- Create a plan for technical advice

Table 1. Number of establishments by size in percentage.

Year	MSMEs (%)	Great industry (%)	Total establishments
1958	96.7	3.3	11,125
1959	96.1	3.9	10,572
1960	95.9	4.1	10,446
1962	95.7	4.3	11,082
1963	95.8	4.2	11,296

Source: Pallares (2002).

- Fix high taxes to imported goods
- Incorporate the wage benefits making the salary process easier and predictable
- Create an industrial bank especially designed for SMEs

In 1964, ACOPI created the Guarantee Fund, aimed at buying and selling industrial raw materials for MSMEs, and to guarantee the credits that companies need to get the raw materials.

Between the 1960s and the 1980s, although the SMEs sector continued its growth process, it still received marginal treatment by governments and state institutions. The contribution to employment grew from 47.5% in 1967 to 50.5% in 1984. Other achievements of this term were:

- The fulfilment of the Stanford mission in 1962, which examined the sector and made recommendations for the development of the SMEs;
- The creation of the Servicio Nacional de Aprendizaje (SENA) established to provide training for operators and managerial personnel. ACOPI had a position on the board of directors and could influence the orientation of the institution;
- The creation of the Corporacion Financiera Popular in 1967 as a financial institution especially focused on providing credits to SMEs. The creation of the Fondo Financiero Industrial and the Fondo de Inversiones Privadas in the Banco de la Republica did provide private banks with a leverage tool for loans to SMEs with governmental resources;
- The creation of the 'Technical and managerial assistance program' by SENA in 1968 aimed to modernize and strengthen the management of SMEs and managerial knowledge improve the operation of the enterprises;
- The issuing of laws allowing the creation of industrial parks;
- The creation within the Banco Popular of the 'Industrial Development Program for Intermediate Cities' which seeks to promote the appearance of new entrepreneurs and new businesses, and the expansion of existing ones in the less developed cities of the country, with the support of 'Industrial Promoters' who provided advise and orientation to the entrepreneurs in their growing process;
- The establishment of the National Guarantee Fund in 1982 to facilitate the process of SME loans;
- The creation of the Advisory Council for SMEs in 1981 within the Ministry of Development (Pallares, 2002).

In 1988, the Congress issued the first law for SMEs, law 78/88. Its main issues were:

- Promote the integral development of SMEs;
- Create a high-level state agency to guide policy and to coordinate the different actions to support SMEs;
- Promote favourable conditions in the institutional environment for its development;
- Support the micro, small and medium enterprises;
- Create an Advisory Council for SMEs at a national level and an SME Division in the Ministry of Development;
- Encourage the government to contract and to purchase from SMEs;

- Encourage private and public banks and the IFI to give increased credit to SMEs;
- Develop tax incentives for job creation and the reinvestment of profits;
- Stimulate in all relevant government agencies, the promotion of exports and the development of alternatives for outsourcing and technical assistance;
- Encourage the formation of industrial parks and business in different regions of the country;
- Promote research in the sector with government resources.

In the late 1970s and early 1980s, the Fundacion Carvajal was leader in recognizing the micro-enterprise sector and led the design of training, counselling, support and guidance for these entities. Its success gave rise to the birth of many foundations and NGOs to support micro-enterprises. The Colombian model quickly spread throughout Latin America. Furthermore, in the early 1980s, INCOLDA developed the programme 'Management for Small and Medium-size Industries', with the intention of professionalizing the managerial activities of SMEs.

In the early 1990s, Colombia began its process of economic opening to the international market (globalization strategy). Together with the serious social, political, economic and security problems that the country was enduring, and a prolonged power rationing, SMEs had to trade in a difficult period as international competitors increased significantly and the business environment was not positive. Gaviria's government (1990–1994) promoted several activities to rectify this situation: Monitor studies to improve competitiveness of different sectors, restructuring of SENA, issuing the law of Science and Technology, creation of the Foreign Trade Bank BANCOLDEX and the Trust for Export Promotion (Proexport), regulations for the operational mechanisms for free zones and for attracting foreign investors (Reina et al., 2013). Thereafter, Samper's government (1994–1998) developed additional activities which included: the creation of the National Competitiveness Council and the National Innovation System, the restructuring IFI to have an orientation towards the MSME sector and the establishment of competitiveness agreements in selected productive chains (Reina et al., 2013). In Pastrana's government (1998–2002), ACOPI's leaders reached key positions in the government and through the Ministry of Commerce managed to push several far-reaching initiatives for the development of SMEs (Reina et al., 2013):

- The guidelines were formulated for policy for entrepreneurship development;
- Law 590 of 2000, known as the SME's act was launched;
- The creation of the Strategic Export Plan (and within this PROEXPORT run the 'Expopyme Program') which aims to prepare Colombian SMEs to export by fortifying the managerial capacity of entrepreneurs and managers and the infrastructure of SMEs;
- Development of the 'Young Entrepreneurs Program' and the CEINFI's Chair (Creation of Enterprise with International Future Impact), to build a mechanism for the emergence of new entrepreneurs in the country;
- Establish the operational stage of the Social Enterprise Development Program (PRODES) that introduces a partnership approach of companies in the same sector.
- The creation of the Business Development Centres in partnership with CONFECAMARAS and IDB to give support and counselling to SMEs;

- Universidad Icesi, with support from the Inter-American Development Bank IDB conceptualized, designed and implemented the 'SME Network Program (Red Pyme)', which allowed the creation of networks of SME enterprises and entrepreneurs linked to a pivot (big) company, aiming to improve the competitiveness of the whole system in which the pivot acted. This project included management training and specialized advisory activities;
- ACOPI in association with Centre for Entrepreneurship Development at the Universidad Icesi organized a business trip to the Asian Tiger countries, which allowed 90 SME entrepreneurs to come into direct contact with developments and entrepreneurs in Taiwan, Singapore, Hong Kong and Malaysia, and begin business operations with them;
- 32 public regional and private committees were created (CARCES) for the development of SMEs, and 41 productive chains were promoted.

Uribe's government (2002–2010) continued with many of these programmes, but added some other activities (Reina et al., 2013):

- The National Policy for Production Transformation was formulated for promoting Small and Medium Enterprises;
- The National Competitiveness system was redesigned;
- Law 905 of 2004 was issued to amend law 590 of 2000;
- New financial instruments were created in BANCOLDEX, National Fund of Guarantees and the Bank of Opportunities;
- New non-financial instruments were created, designed and get into operational phases to encourage entrepreneurship, to promote innovation and technological development, to facilitate access to markets and to support the processes of human resource training;
- Law 1014 of 2016 was issued aimed at promoting the culture of entrepreneurship, including regulations of the Fondo Emprender oriented to provide seed capital for new businesses;
- A programme of developing an entrepreneurial culture was designed;
- FOMIPYME and COLCIENCIAS's programmes were strengthen, and were orientated to stimulate research, technological development and innovation for SMEs;
- SENA was developed to improve the specialized and technical training of human resources;
- A new programme by EXPOPYME was developed for 'Exporting Enterprise Networks';
- The GEM research was started in Colombia with support from Universidad Icesi, Universidad Javeriana, Universidad de los Andes and Universidad del Norte;
- There was increased stimulation of the domestic market by public procurement;
- Implementation of a system to simplify procedures for the creation and operation of SMEs;
- Development of programmes for the implementation of ICT in SMEs;
- Formulation of the Production Transformation Policy and the definition of 16 economic sectors selected as the leading sectors for Colombian Development;
- Creation of the Regional Councils for the Micro, Small and Medium enterprises;
- Encouragement for the formalization of entrepreneurial activity;
- Strengthening of the development of non-financial market for business development;

- Universidad Icesi started the process of adaptation and adjustment of the model of the Small Business Development Center in Colombia through the creation of the Centro Alaya;
- Interactive work between University – Industry and the offices of research and results innovation were created (OTRIS);
- The intellectual property registration system was strengthened;
- Incentives for production development and business partnerships were generated.

In Santos's governments (2010–2016), the following activities have been undertaken (Reina et al., 2013):

- INNpulsa was created to stimulate the production sectors of the country and to get more innovators and entrepreneurs to venture into high economic impact processes for Colombia;
- Formulation and operational phases of the Promotion Plan for Prosperity and Employment, which provides financial support for small and medium companies that want to enter new markets and/or develop new products;
- The sheltered sectors under the Production Transformation Plan was widened;
- Selection of the 'Locomotives' for Colombian development;
- A law that defined new distribution rules for oil and mining royalties was issued allowing direct resources for business innovation processes and for the development of SMEs;
- SENA's role in the human talent development process was readjusted;
- An intensive programme to improve Colombian's road infrastructure and communications was developed;
- Several free trade agreements were signed;
- A policy of clustering was prioritized;
- The programme of business and labour was strengthened;
- The National System Competitiveness in Science, Technology and Innovation was created;
- The Production Development Program, Science, Technology and Innovation was established;
- The Apps.co program, an entrepreneurial development project, supported by MinTIC to develop Technological Entrepreneur, was designed and implemented;
- Support Centres to Technology and Innovation were created;
- The model of the Small Business Development Centre, orientated to support micro and small enterprises in the birth and consolidation's stages, was expanded to several cities of the country;
- Private and Public Capital Funds were developed to support new businesses and existing ones;
- The programme 'aProgresar', a BANCOLDEX initiative for the development of entrepreneur and manager of SMEs, was expanded to several cities;
- A plan to improve the productivity of micro-enterprises was designed;
- Agreements were strengthened between Chambers of Commerce and the Cajas de Compensacion Familiar for business development;
- Favourable tax mechanisms for new companies were established;

- New legal figures for the business creation process were created;
- The National Training System for Work and for Human Development was consolidated;
- The education system started to improve its path for student entrepreneurs with scholarships and financial aids for good students;
- A Tax Simplification for SMEs was implemented;
- The National Program of Industrial Design was applied;
- The INNOVA Award was designed.

It is important to recognize that while many initiatives were introduced, not all of them were successful. Indeed, the level of success for such initiatives have varied widely from hugely successful to unsuccessful depending on the measures that a policy-maker might employ to assess the level of impact of the initiative.

Colombian SMEs today

The Colombian Business and Social Registry believes that there are now 2.2 million establishments in the country that are formalized businesses (Revista Coyuntura PyME, 2016). Of this total, 94.7% are micro-enterprises, 4.9% are small and medium enterprises, and 0.4% are large companies, which confirm the importance of SMEs in Colombia's business structure. According to Colombian law:

- Micro-enterprises are those with less than 10 employees, and less than 501 monthly legal minimum wages in assets;
- Small ones are those between 11 and 50 employees and assets between 501 and 5001 monthly legal minimum wages in assets;
- Medians are those with between 51 and 200 employees and assets between 5001 and 15,000 monthly legal minimum wages;
- Large are those with more than 200 employees and above 15,000 active monthly legal minimum wages in assets.

DANE (National Administrative Department of Statistics) found that SMEs account for 67% of employment, contributing 28% to GDP boosting national productivity in all sectors. In the field of exports, the participation of SMEs is also significant as they represent 83% of the total export companies and 61% of the companies that export goods with high technological content (Dominguez, 2016). However, in international trade, Colombian SMEs contribution is only 5% of the total value of exports (ProColombia 2014).

It is known that in Colombia, 26% of the SMEs have been around for more than 22 years, 28% between 10 and 22 years, 22% between 6 and 10 years, and 24% less than 6 years. Approximately, 70% of the SME companies have maintained over the years the same economic activity with which they began their operation, indicating that very few have been strongly orientated towards expanding their portfolios. More than 50% of the Colombian SMEs are family business, but most of them have not made significant development in the construction of specific management tools for family business, such as family protocols (Londoño, 2016). Regarding the management of the SMEs, 70% are men; most of them are aged between 46 and 65 years, over 50% have college degrees and about 20% have postgraduate degrees. Meanwhile, 59% of managers were also the owners of the company (Londoño, 2016). In research done by the FAEDPyME Network in Colombia in 2012, several important facts were identified about the Colombian SMEs (Gálvez, Cuellar, Restrepo, Bernal, & Cortez, 2014).

- The average age for companies was 21.1 years;
- The average age of owners and managers was 51.3 years;
- 70.1% of SMEs in Colombia were run by men;
- 76.5% of SMEs were family businesses;
- 52.6% of companies were constituted as a corporation;
- 42.8% of companies were headed by a manager whose level of education was technological or lower level, 44.1% were at the university level and 13.7% had graduate degrees;
- The average number of employees in Colombian SMEs was 29.8 in 2011 and 31 in 2012;
- Only 13% of SMEs had exported during the 2012 and they accounted for 25.4% of their total sales volume;
- 44.5% of the companies felt that the business environment in which the activity took place had remained the same as the previous year, while 38.8% thought it had improved and 16.7% considered that it had worsened;
- 52% of SMEs has made formal strategic planning, but 78.8% did so to one-year time horizon;
- The SMEs made cooperation agreements as follows: 29.1% for purchasing and procurement processes, 27.2% for marketing, 20.6% for logistics, 20.3% for production and 14.9% for research and development;
- 16.3% of SMEs have been involved in cooperation programmes with universities, 14.5% with government agencies and 3.9% with NGOs;
- The department of accounting and finance was the most common in all types of companies, followed by marketing, operations and purchasing, quality, human resources, and finally research and development;
- Only 30% of small businesses considered that they were using a strong and modern technology enough to compete;
- A very low percentage of SMEs had ISO quality certification (31.2% of the medium size, 18% of the small and just 2.5% of the micro-enterprises);
- In innovation, the most frequent activities were: changes or improvements in production processes and services (58.8%), acquisition of new equipment (50%), marketing of new products or services (47.6%), changes or improvements in the areas of marketing and sales (44.6%), changes and improvements in purchasing and supply (45.1%), and changes and improvements in governance and management (36.1%);
- Regarding the use of web pages, corporate internet and digital marketing, it was found that 85%, 64.6% and 55%, respectively of the medium-sized enterprises used them. Among small enterprises, the use frequencies were 64.7%, 39.2% and 41.7%, respectively, while for micro-enterprises, the use frequencies were 22.8%, 12.2% and 21.8%, respectively;
- In relation to the use of financial accounting tools, the most used were management information systems, implementation of cost accounting, budget control, financial and economic analysis and internal audit.

- In relation to the volume of financing that they used, 20.4% of the enterprises believe that there had been an increase in financing and 28.1% considered that there had been a decrease in the financing resources used;
- The cost of funding had increased for 18.8% of the firms and decreased for 20.5% of the firms;
- Warranties needed to access finance had increased in 17.6% of cases and decreased in 16.8%;
- Surprisingly, 61% of SMEs stated that they did not ask for a loan because the company did not need it;
- The competitive advantages of the companies that received the highest scores were more satisfied customer, higher quality products, capacity to adapt to changes to the market (flexibility) and efficient internal processes;
- The factors that positively influence the performance or success of the company are:
  - The size of the company;
  - The use of formal strategic planning;
  - Having a manager with higher level of studies;
  - Co-operation agreements with other companies and development agencies;
  - Have a strong technological position;
  - Have accounting systems, budgetary and financial control;
  - Use the reinvestment of profits and suppliers as a source of funding.

These findings offer an excellent profile of Colombian SMEs and give greater understanding to their strengths and weaknesses at the time of the survey.

Current actions for SMEs

There are many options for improving Colombian SMEs, and it is obvious that there is a requirement to continue designing and implementing specific programmes to address the various shortcomings that they face. Among the challenges are the following:

- Training at all levels,
- The implementation of quality standards,
- Improvements in productivity,
- Building business networks and clusters,
- R&D activity that leads to the generation of innovation in product process management, etc.;
- Optimizing financing systems,
- Expanding markets in the national context,
- Export promotions that allow companies to expand markets and their production levels,
- Generating stable rules that permit them to adequately plan their development,
- Obtaining environmental certifications,
- The launch of innovative products.

To adequately address this set of requirements is quite difficult, especially given the low level of resources that the Colombian Government has dedicated traditionally to support this sector.

The Colombian Government is faced with a situation where is must consider what is appropriate to create a modern industrial policy for Colombia consisting of a battery of cross-cutting strategies and other sectoral strategies, each with programmes, instruments and entities working articulately, with a regional approach and an institutional framework to promote competitiveness and innovation (Ministerio de Comercio, Industria y Turismo, 2014). Crossing the system, there are strategies such as entrepreneurship, innovation, business formalization, conquering the domestic market, and regulatory actions aimed at improving the environment to facilitate the creation and development of enterprises. On the other hand, the vertical component of the policy includes those strategies aimed at specific sectors with the capacity to lead growth and job creation in other sectors of the economy. In this set are the Production Transformation Program, the Committee on Industry, and strategies for strengthening and promoting clusters and production chains. The current Colombian policy includes four pillars, each of them with specific actions for SMEs with a central objective so that Colombian companies can compete and grow, creating jobs and economic prosperity for the country.

First pillar: development of productivity

(1) Business modernization – with good credit conditions (low cost, easier warranties, good payment schedules) through Bancóldex credit; deferral of import tariffs for competitive access to capital goods; development of suppliers for modernization through iNNpulsa Mipyme;
(2) Innovation and entrepreneurship – with royalties for innovation and seed capital through iNNpulsa; tax benefits for entrepreneurship and innovation; strengthening the industrial property system;
(3) Human capital – transforming the training offer in alliance with SENA and the Ministry of Education, to be relevant to the needs of the production sectors, specifically the Production Transformation Program;
(4) Formalizing Business – with tax incentives through the Law of Employment Generation and Formalizing, and programmes such as the Brigades for Formalizing.

Second pillar: transformation of production sectors and regions, and promotion of production linkages

(1) The Production Transformation Programme – which now has 20 sectors;
(2) Development of Clusters – with programmes such as competitive routes through iNNpulsa, to support regions for the development of their production potential;
(3) Business Networks – with programmes like iNNpulsa Mipymes or formal Chains;
(4) Promotion of the Internal Market – with the Buy Colombian' programme that runs in partnership with Propaís;
(5) Public Procurement – in alliance with Agencia Colombiana de Compras Eficientes (ACCE) (Colombian agency of effective purchasing) to promote domestic purchases in the procurement processes of central and local governments.

Third pillar: internationalization of businesses and consumers

(1) Preferential access to more consumers – through a wide network of trade agreements;
(2) Explorers of foreign markets – with the support of the Centros de Aprovechamiento and the Free Trade Agreements, making the Colombian business person an active part of regional and global value chains;
(3) Export promotion and investment management – in support with Proexport;
(4) Quality and consumer protection – by strengthening the National Quality Subsystem and the Superintendence of Industry and Commerce.

Fourth pillar: country competitiveness

(1) Obtain stable macroeconomic conditions – low inflation and favourable exchange rate for the production development;
(2) Improvement of connectivity and infrastructure;
(3) Continuance of production costs reduction – energy and gas, tax and labour costs;
(4) Ensure fair competition – avoiding smuggling and dumping.

This industrial policy is coordinated at the highest level, by the National System for Competitiveness and Innovation (SNCeI) as a framework that integrates formally and coherently, as well as incorporating all the efforts of public and private institutions and academia, in the formulation, implementation and monitoring of the policies affecting competitiveness. With the development of these actions, it will be possible to give a significant boost to SMEs in their competitiveness and through it enhance the production contribution of the country. To achieve that ambition, dynamism will need to be present in all economic and social processes and in this way, improve the country socio-economic indicators.

Conclusions

In the past 70 years of recognized action concerning Colombian SMEs, it is possible to identify several highlights:

- The importance and positioning that SMEs and entrepreneurs have acquired in the Colombian business community;
- Their role in the generation of multiple institutions, offices, commissions, laws, programmes and projects aimed at the harmonious development of SMEs;
- The changes in policy used over the years to improve the creation and development of more and better enterprises;
- The role of entrepreneurs who through their associations have promoted various laws, policies and projects to achieve better supporting mechanisms;
- The positive attitude of governments that have promoted the formulation of policies to support SMEs;
- The growth in the sector, even in the Colombian environment, which over the years has been affected by sensitive phenomena (such as violence, internal war, corruption, drug trafficking, insecurity, legal instability), which demonstrates the resourcefulness and resilience of the Colombian entrepreneurs;

- The need for specialized academic programmes in the management of SMEs and in the birth and development of new and existing businesses, to give owners and managers an appropriate view of their sector and develop entrepreneurial skills which are necessary for the survival and growth of the enterprises;
- The need to initiate research programmes on the future of SMEs, especially research, aimed at assessing the achievement of growth targets and identifying the factors that enabled this achievement.

The challenge for Colombian policy-makers is what future initiatives should they prioritize given the limited resources of any government and how will they measure the impact of any initiatives that they might introduce. Using the OECD Framework is a useful tool to help sort through the gaps and overlaps that might exist in terms of the current ecosystem, and it can also serve as a mechanism to explain to the electorate what it is seeking to achieve with any new plans it will introduce. While so much has been achieved over the past 70 years, the question now is 'What next in terms of supporting Colombian SMEs?'

Disclosure statement

No potential conflict of interest was reported by the author.

References

Asociación Colombiana de Medianas y Pequeñas Industrias. (n.d.) *Archivo ACOPI (1951–2000).* Bogotá DC.

Dominguez, J. (2016, April 23). *Ser pequeño cuenta.* Periódico El País. Retrieved from http://www. elpais.com.co/elpais/opinion/columna/julian-dominguez-rivera/ser-pequeno-cuenta

Gálvez, E., Cuellar, K., Restrepo, C., Bernal, C., & Cortez, J. (2014). *Análisis estratégico para el desarrollo de las MiPyme Colombianas.* Cali: Universidad del Valle.

Garay, L. (n.d.). *Colombia: estructura industrial e internacionalización 1967–1996.* Biblioteca Luis Ángel Arango. Banco de La República de Colombia. Retrieved from http://www. banrepcultural.org/blaavirtual/economia/industrilatina/058.htm

Londoño, D. (2016). *Caracterización del segmento PyME diferencias a nivel regional.* Revista Coyuntura Pyme. Ed. 52. Bogotá DC.

Ministerio de Comercio, Industria y Turismo. (2014). *La política industrial durante el gobierno del presidente Juan Manuel Santos.* Bogotá D.C. Retrieved from http://www.mincit.gov.co/loader. php?lServicio=Documentos&lFuncion=verPdf&id=70157&name=Libro_Politica_Industrial_ Juan_Manuel_Santos_balance_a_Ago-2013.pdf&prefijo=file

OECD. (2014). *Entrepreneurship at a glance 2014.* Paris: Author.

Pallares, Z. (2002). *ACOPI el gremio de la PYME, cincuenta años de historia (1952–2001).* In *Empresas y empresarios en la historia de Colombia. Siglos XIX–XX. Una colección de estudios recientes.* Tomo II. Grupo Editorial Norma, Universidad de los Andes, CEPAL, pp. 1147–1188. Bogotá, DC.

Reina, M., Castro F., & Tamayo L. (2013). *20 años de políticas de competitividad en Colombia.* FEDESARROLLO, Bogotá, DC. Retrieved from http://www.fedesarrollo.org.co/wp-content/ uploads/2011/08/20-a%C3%B1os-de-pol%C3%ADticas-de-competitividad-en-Colombia-Informe-BID-Competitividad-Dic-19-13-FINAL.pdf

Revista Coyuntura Pyme. (2016). *Tamaño de las empresas en Colombia.* Comentario Económico. Ed. 52. Bogotá, DC.

World Bank. (2016). *Doing business report.* Washington, DC: Author.

Does 'entrepreneurship' exist?

Simon Bridge

ABSTRACT

The word 'entrepreneurship' appears to have been coined in the early twentieth century. Later, because there was a word for it and, following Birch's identification of small businesses as the creators of net new jobs, because there was perceived to be a need for it, people came to believe that a deterministic condition called entrepreneurship existed. To establish its credibility, especially as an academic subject, researchers have sought to define it and establish how it operates – but this search has produced more questions than answers and has neither uniquely defined it nor identified its 'rules'. Therefore, it should probably be concluded that it does not exist as the condition that people have conceived it to be – and consequently one should stop using the word because it serves to confuse, mislead and misdirect.

Introduction – the invention of the word

According to popular interpretation of economic history, it was an Irishman, Richard Cantillon, who introduced the French word 'entrepreneur' into the economic lexicon through the posthumous publication in 1754 of his book *Essai sur la nature du commerce en général*. The French had used the word before that time, but not as Cantillon did to describe an actor within the economic system. However, the English-speaking world was slow to take up this usage and, in a translation of Cantillon's work in 1930, Higgs used the word 'undertaker' as the nearest English equivalent. Nevertheless, the word entrepreneur did enter the English language – even to the extent that President George W. Bush was once reputed to have accused the French of not having a word for it.

However, the word 'entrepreneurship' does appear to be an English-speaking invention, probably first used in the 1920s or early 1930s, and which was formed by adding 'ship' to the word entrepreneur. Initially, it may have referred to no more than entrepreneurs doing what entrepreneurs do in creating new enterprises (Low & MacMillan, 1988) but, with the suffix 'ship', entrepreneurship began to be viewed as some sort of condition which entrepreneurs shared – and this condition was one which was associated with, and contributed to, economy development (e.g. Cole, 1942). In time, the word became more widely accepted which encouraged a belief that, because there was a word for it, entrepreneurship must exist and therefore 'entrepreneurship' began to be researched and taught. Indeed, it has been claimed that deliberate entrepreneurship education started as early as 1938 in Japan (Hannon, 2005).

The search for entrepreneurship

A big boost to the popularity of the concept came in 1979 when Birch released the results of his research into employment in the USA (Birch, 1979) in which he concluded that it was small firms which created the majority of additional new jobs. As he put it two years later:

> Of all the net new jobs created in our sample of 5.6 million businesses between 1969 and 1976, two-thirds were created by firms with twenty or fewer employees and about 80 percent were created by firms with 100 or fewer employees. (Birch, 1981)

This identification of small businesses as the net creators of new jobs came at a time of rising unemployment in many countries. As a result, governments which were anxious to address this issue wanted more small businesses, and in turn this required more entrepreneurs to create them. Therefore, governments wanted something which would encourage more entrepreneurs and 'entrepreneurship' appeared to be that condition. So, having invented the word, people came to believe that a condition called entrepreneurship existed, not only because there was a word for it, but also because people wanted it to exist (especially following the work of Birch).

Clearly, many governments wanted to encourage more entrepreneurs to start a business and made budgets available to do that. In turn, many in academia wanted both to please governments and to access those budgets, so 'entrepreneurship' research and education increased. However, those engaged in this work also wanted academic credibility. In 1989 Bygrave commented that, if entrepreneurship 'is to grow in stature as a separate discipline, it will need to develop its own distinct methods and theories', while in 2000 Shane and Venkataraman declared that:

> For a field of social science to have usefulness, it must have a conceptual framework that explains and predicts a set of empirical phenomena not explained or predicted by conceptual frameworks already in existence in other fields.

Thus, as a foundation for building its credibility as a social science, two key assumptions appear to have been made regarding entrepreneurship:

(1) That entrepreneurship exists as a specific discrete identifiable phenomenon which somehow produces more and/or better entrepreneurs;
(2) That this phenomenon is deterministic in that it operates in a consistent way in accordance with 'rules' which can be identified and from which its behaviour can then be predicted.

These assumptions have in turn provided a focus for academic research to identify and define this phenomenon and to establish the frameworks or 'rules' governing its operation. Initially, it appeared that progress was being made as Plaschka (1992) observed that in the late 1970s (when Birch reported) entrepreneurship had been a tangible activity, academically flaky and lacking in a scholarly body of knowledge and that 'little research in entrepreneurship [went] on and consequently the literature on it remained thin'. However, he reported that since then, not only had there been 'a dramatic increase in the entrepreneurship literature', but also there was 'a positive movement toward a commonly accepted definition of entrepreneurship and toward the definition of the boundaries of the field of entrepreneurship'.

But that accepted definition has not yet emerged and, instead of answers, it appears that this search has found more questions. For instance, there are still many different uses and definitions of entrepreneurship of which the following a just a sample:

(1) According to Stevenson (2004), 'entrepreneurship is the pursuit of opportunity beyond the resources you currently control'.
(2) Gibb (2000) suggested that 'entrepreneurship relates to ways in which people, in all kinds of organizations, behave in order to cope with and take advantage of uncertainty and complexity and how in turn this becomes embodied in: ways of doing things; ways of seeing things; ways of feeling things; ways of communicating things; and ways of learning things'.
(3) Baumol (1990) defined 'entrepreneurs … simply, to be persons who are ingenious and creative in finding ways that add to their own wealth, power, and prestige' and implied that entrepreneurship refers to such people operating in any area of life.
(4) Jasinski, Nehrt, O'Connor, and Simione (2003) asserted that 'one of the major objectives of entrepreneurship education is to provide students with the necessary skills to design, create, launch and effectively manage a business'.
(5) Hytti and Kuopusjärvi (2004) have suggested that there are different roles which might be assigned to entrepreneurship education programmes depending on what aim was being pursued. One of the aims they identify is learning to become entrepreneurial (an approach which is consistent with a wider interpretation of entrepreneurship), whereas another aim is that of learning to become an entrepreneur (which is generally interpreted as learning how to start a business).
(6) Zacharakis, Bygrave, and Shepherd (2000) stated that the Global Entrepreneurship Monitor (GEM) definition of entrepreneurship has been 'any attempt to create a new business enterprise or to expand an existing business by an individual, a team of individuals or an established business'.
(7) Gabr and Hoffmann (2006) in Denmark defined entrepreneurship specifically as 'the entry and creation of high-growth firms'.

These descriptions are not only different, but some are not even consistent with others. So, there still is no single widely accepted definition of entrepreneurship (or even of an entrepreneur), but instead many definitions and uses exist, some of which contradict others, and which together lead to confusion and misdirection. If people cannot even define what they are searching for, it should not be surprising that people have also not been able to identify the 'rules' by which this undefined condition operates. Therefore, the reality is that, after a considerable search, people have not been able to confirm either of the key assumptions indicated above.

Elephant or artichokes?

There is a story of three people who were blindfolded and then each asked to feel an object and say what they thought it was. It was actually an elephant, but the person who felt its trunk identified it as a hose, the one who felt the ear identified it as a fan, and the third who felt a leg identified it as tree. Nevertheless, despite the elephant having been identified as different things, these were all related parts of the same object. Further, once it is clear that they are all parts of an elephant, then how each part will behave can be predicted from an understanding of elephants and how they move and operate.

But what about artichokes? Apparently on the basis of taste, Globe artichokes, Jerusalem artichokes and Chinese artichokes are all called artichokes. However, the bits that are eaten are the base of the flower bud of a globe artichoke, the tubers growing on the roots of a Jerusalem artichoke and the tuberous underground stems of a Chinese artichoke. Despite the similarity in taste, they are not related. Globe artichokes are a variety of thistle, Jerusalem artichokes are related to sunflowers (and are called 'Jerusalem' supposedly as a corruption of 'girasole' – the Italian word for sunflower) and Chinese artichokes are a perennial herb of the mint family. Tasting the same and being called artichokes do not make them the same thing.

The things that have variously been labelled 'entrepreneurship', while apparently having some similar aspects, are hard to identify as being the same phenomenon. However, is that because they are essentially the same elephant (but not enough research has been done to establish the connection) or because they are in reality more like different artichokes sharing no more than a similar taste? It is the suggestion of this paper that people have researched widely, but because a common elephant link has not been found, the artichoke analogy is better and therefore one should consider the conclusion that entrepreneurship does not exist as the single, objectively distinguishable behaviour that it is supposed to be. If this is the case then trying to agree, or impose, a single definition of entrepreneurship will not be productive and continuing to insist that entrepreneurship as variously defined is all the same thing will be counterproductive.

What should we do?

Should the possibility be addressed that entrepreneurship does not exist (as the condition it is supposed it to be) and, if so, should the word 'entrepreneurship' be abandoned because:

- The use of the word is confusing as it can have different and sometimes conflicting meanings or associations. That leads to problems as when different sides of a discussion or debate assume different meanings (e.g. Bridge, Hegarty, & Porter, 2010).
- Even if the possibility of different meanings is acknowledged, the use of the same term can nevertheless lead to false parallels being drawn. An example of this, also from the field of entrepreneurship education, is that even when it is acknowledged that entrepreneurship as 'enterprise-for-new-venture creation' courses differ from entrepreneurship as 'enterprise-for-life' courses, it sometimes appears to be assumed that they have sufficient in common to use the same course content (Bridge & Hegarty, 2016).
- Because the word carries the suffix '-ship', it will continue to lead to an expectation that it is more than just a label for an activity and instead indicates a common and deterministic condition – like membership or leadership.

Doing nothing is not going to resolve the problem and neither is trying to redefine entrepreneurship going to work. However, any one person who drops the use of the word is likely to be more meaningful in their communication as they would have to find other words to use in its place. That might require more careful thought about the different meanings intended so that the alternative words chosen might then be clearer and less confusing.

Examples of misdirection

Recognizing that entrepreneurship does not exist might also have benefits in economic thinking if it alters the general understanding about the source of entrepreneurial behaviour and the conditions that foster economic growth. Has the belief in the existence of entrepreneurship as a condition which somehow generates entrepreneurs misdirected policy-makers and academics, and encouraged people to think that if an economy wants more entrepreneurs, then the seed of entrepreneurship needs to be planted within individuals because that will somehow grow an entrepreneurial tendency within them? Is this why policy-makers and academics have sought to do this by programmes targeting individuals through courses, support schemes, advice, tax benefits, mentors and other encouragements to build their entrepreneurship? But entrepreneurship policies based on such methods have not worked (Bridge & O'Neill, 2013) and it has been suggested that that is because, instead of being in individuals, an entrepreneurial ethos is located within society and particularly in the peer influence of people's social circles (e.g. Bridge, 2010). This was what Baumol was saying when he suggested that what made a society entrepreneurial what not the proportion of entrepreneurial people but whether the 'rules' of that society encouraged those people to apply it productively or not (Baumol, 1990). Thus, as in many aspects of life, individuals respond to social influence much more than individual inclination:

> The notion that we are rational individuals who respond to information by making decisions consciously, consistently and independently is, at best, a very partial account of who we are. A wide body of scientific knowledge is now telling us what many have long intuitively sensed – humans are a fundamentally social species, formed through and for social interaction. (Rowson & McGilchrist, 2013)

Therefore, it is suggested, a belief in the existence of 'entrepreneurship' has led people to look for the source of entrepreneurial activity in the wrong place – but has that belief also led people to look for it as a cause rather than an effect? As the introduction to this paper indicates, from the time the word appears to have been coined, entrepreneurship has been seen as the key factor in economic development. Thus, it has been seen as some sort of magic potion (the hoped-for ingredient the application of which could cure weak or failing economies) and that has been the main reason for seeking it. As has been observed: 'when policy makers and other observers emphasise the role of entrepreneurship, they almost exclusively focus on its role as a generator of jobs, economic growth and wealth' (Henrekson, 2014).

But what does lead to economic growth? One of the clearest examples in history must be the Industrial Revolution but entrepreneurship rarely features among the many factors suggested as explanations for why it happened when and where it did. A wide variety of conditions have been suggested including the following: cheap energy but high wage rates (Allen, 2009); favourable natural resources, Protestant non-conformism, applied science and mechanical ability and the availability of capital (Mathias, 1983); the application of open and independently fostered science (Lipsey, Carlaw, & Bekar, 2005), a willingness of those with capital and/or entrepreneurial talent to invest it in 'business' (Baumol, 1990); and an 'inclusive legal regime which protected individual ownership of the results from expropriation by others (Acemoglu & Robinson, 2013). However, a study of the various accounts on offer does not identify an injection of 'entrepreneurship' as a sufficient, or even as a necessary, contributory cause.

Productive entrepreneurs do appear to have been part of the Industrial Revolution and these entrepreneurs started businesses which created wealth and employed people. A belief in 'entrepreneurship' as a factor in economic growth could lead one to focus on those businesses and at the people (entrepreneurs) who created them, but in doing that one would miss the reasons why the Industrial Revolution occurred where and when it did. Is it therefore the case that, instead of being one of the factors that needed to be in place for the Industrial Revolution to happen, productive entrepreneurial activity in any form was something that happened when the relevant factors all came together? Instead of being an ingredient which could be added to create the conditions necessary, was it actually created by those conditions? Was it a product of the process, not a cause of it?

Conclusion

This review suggests not only that entrepreneurship does not exist as the condition people have supposed it to be, but that its supposed existence has led to errors such as looking for the source of entrepreneurial activity in the wrong place and seeing such activity as a condition necessary for economic growth instead of being the result of such conditions. Thus, overall, the continuing belief in, and the use of, the term has served to:

- confuse – because of its mixed meanings,
- mislead – because it implies a condition which does not exist, and
- misdirect – because it has led people to look in the wrong place for the things they do want.

This indicates that entrepreneurship is not only an invented concept and a myth, but also that its use as a term is very unhelpful. Therefore, people should abandon the concept and stop using the word.

Note: A fuller explanation of all these points is provided in Bridge (2017).

Disclosure statement

No potential conflict of interest was reported by the author.

References

Acemoglu, D., & Robinson, J. (2013). *Why nations fail.* London: Profile Books.

Allen, R. C. (2009). *The British Industrial Revolution in global perspective.* Cambridge: Cambridge University Press.

Baumol, W. J. (1990). Entrepreneurship: Productive, unproductive, and destructive. *Journal of Political Economy, 98*(5, pt.1), 893–921.

Birch, D. L. (1979). *The job generation process (Unpublished report prepared for the Economic Development Administration).* Cambridge, MA: MIT Program on Neighborhood and Regional Change.

Birch, D. L. (1981). Who creates jobs? *The Public Interest, 65,* 7.

Bridge, S. (2010). *Rethinking enterprise policy.* Basingstoke: Palgrave Macmillan.

Bridge, S. (2017). *The search for entrepreneurship: Finding more questions than answers.* London: Routledge.

Bridge, S., & Hegarty, C. (2016). Reconceptualising curriculum design for entrepreneurship in higher education. *AISHE-J, 8*(1, Spring), 2411–2414.

Bridge, S., Hegarty, C., & Porter, S. (2010). Rediscovering enterprise: Developing appropriate university entrepreneurship education. *Education + Training, 52*(8/9), 722–734.

Bridge, S., & O'Neill, K. (2013). *Understanding enterprise, entrepreneurship and small business.* Basingstoke: Palgrave.

Bygrave, W. (1989). The entrepreneurship paradigm (I): A philosophical look at its methodologies. *Entrepreneurship: Theory and Practice, 14*(1), 7–26.

Cantillon, R. (1754). *Essai sur la nature du commerce en général.* Edited with an English translation and other material by H. Higgs. London: Frank Cass & Co Ltd. 1959 - reissued for the Royal Economic Society.

Cole, A. H. (1942). Entrepreneurship as an area of research. *The Journal of Economic History, 2*(supplement), 118–126.

Gabr, H. M., & Hoffmann, A. (2006, April). *A general policy framework for entrepreneurship.* Copenhagen, Denmark: FORA (Ministry of Economic and Business Affairs' Division for Research and Analysis).

Gibb, A. A. (2000). SME policy, academic research and the growth of ignorance, mythical concepts, myths, assumptions, rituals and confusions. *International Small Business Journal, 18*(3), 13–35.

Hannon, D. (2005). Philosophies of enterprise and entrepreneurship education and the challenges for higher education in the UK. *The International Journal of Entrepreneurship and Innovation, 6*(2), 105–114.

Henrekson, M. (2014, January). *Entrepreneurship, innovation and human flourishing* (IFN Working Paper No.999), p. 2. Stockholm: Research Institute of Industrial Economics.

Higgs, H. (1930). *English translation and editing of Cantillon R. (1754). Essai sur la nature du commerce en général.* London: Frank Cass & Co Ltd. 1959 - reissued for the Royal Economic Society.

Hytti, U., & Kuopusjärvi, P. (2004). *Evaluating and measuring entrepreneurship and enterprise education.* Turku, Finland: Small Business Institute, Turku School of Economics and Business Administration.

Jasinski, D. W., Nehrt, C., O'Connor, M., & Simione, K. (2003). A new approach to integrated entrepreneurship education. *Paper at the ICSB 48th World Conference,* Belfast, June 2003.

Lipsey, R. G., Carlaw, K. I., & Bekar, C. T. (2005). *Economic transformations.* Oxford: Oxford University Press.

Low, M. B., & MacMillan, I. C. (1988). Entrepreneurship: Past research and future challenges. *Journal of Management, 14*(2), 139–161.

Mathias, P. (1983). *The first industrial nation.* London: Methuen.

Plaschka, G. R. (1992). ICSB Senior Vice President, writing in the Bulletin of the International Council for Small Business, XXIV(1, Winter).

Rowson, J., & McGilchrist, I. (2013). *Divided brain, divided world*. London: RSA.

Shane, S., & Venkataraman, S. (2000). The promise of entrepreneurship as a field of research. *Academy of Management Review, 25*(1), 217–226.

Stevenson, H. H. (2004). Intellectual foundations of entrepreneurship. In H. P. Welsch (Ed.), *Entrepreneurship: The way ahead*, (p. 3–14). New York, NY: Routledge.

Zacharakis, A. L., Bygrave, W. D., & Shepherd, D. A. (2000). *Global entrepreneurship monitor United States of America 2000 Executive Report* (p. 5). Kansas City, MO: Kauffman Centre for Entrepreneurial Leadership at the Ewing Marion Kauffmann Foundation.

Index

Abbott, Tony 58
ABS *see* Australian Bureau of Statistics (ABS)
Accelerated Cost Recovery System (ACRS) 32
ACOPI *see* Asociación Colombiana de Pequeñas Industrias (ACOPI)
ACRS *see* Accelerated Cost Recovery System (ACRS)
Affordable Care Act 27, 30–1, 32, 36
agenda shift, business policy: issues never appeared 27–9; small-business voice 26–7
America Invents Act (AIA) 33, 34
American Bar Association's Administrative Law 30
American small business policy 25
ANZCERTA *see* Australia–New Zealand Closer Economic Relations Trade Agreement (ANZCERTA)
Arshed, N. 11, 15
artichokes 123–4
ASBFEO *see* Australian Small Business and Family Enterprise Ombudsman (ASBFEO)
ASIO Building report 105
Asociación Colombiana de Pequeñas Industrias (ACOPI) 109, 110
Australian Bureau of Statistics (ABS) 49
Australia–New Zealand Closer Economic Relations Trade Agreement (ANZCERTA) 49
Australian Small Business and Family Enterprise Ombudsman (ASBFEO) 58
Australian Small Business Commissioner 98–100, 105
Australia small business policy: agricultural commodities 52; Backing Australia's Ability report 58; Beddall Report of 1990 54; Cutler Report of 2008 58; development of 53; economic crisis, 1970s 54; economic history 51; economic transition 1970 to 2015 51–3; "Enterprise Workshop" 55; Independent Contractor's Act, 2006 58; Karpin Report of 1995 55; model business framework 100, 101; New Enterprise Incentive Scheme 1986 54; OPEC oil crisis of 1973 52; *Powering Ideas* 58; recession of 1982–1983 54; small business sector in 49–50; Trade Practices Act, 2006 58

Banco Popular 109
Barclays Bank 84
Baumol, W. J. 123, 125
BDBs *see* Business Development Boards (BDBs)
BECs *see* Business Enterprise Centres (BECs)
Beddall Report of 1990 54
Bennett, R. J. 10, 45, 48
Billson, Bruce 58
Birch, D. L. 24, 25, 122
"BIZ Programme" 57
Blackburn, R. A. 22
Blackford, M. G. 47
Blair Administration 16
BMNZ *see* Business Mentors New Zealand (BMNZ)
Bolger, Jim 55
Bolton, J. E. 47, 48
Brown, Gordon 21
Brown, R. 48
Bush, George W. 121
Business Development Boards (BDBs) 54
Business Enterprise Centres (BECs) 55
Business Mentors New Zealand (BMNZ) 57
business-to-business report 99
Bygrave, W. D. 123

Cameron, A. 50
Cantillon, Richard 121
Carter, S. 11
carve-out principle 30
CCP *see* Chinese Community Party (CCP)
CER *see* Closer Economic Relations (CER)
Chinese Community Party (CCP) 48
Clark, Helen 57
Closer Economic Relations (CER) 51
Coad, A. 85, 87
Colombia small-medium-sized enterprises: Colombian law 115–17; country competitiveness 119; designing and implementing 117–18; historical development 109–15; internationalization 119; modern industrial policy 118; pre-Columbian cultures 109; production sectors, transformation 118;

For Product Safety Concerns and Information please contact our EU
representative GPSR@taylorandfrancis.com
Taylor & Francis Verlag GmbH, Kaufingerstraße 24, 80331 München, Germany